ESCAPE THE RAT RACE
GOD'S WAY

DISCOVER BIBLICAL SECRETS THAT CAN UNLOCK YOUR PATH TO FINANCIAL FREEDOM

Pastor Allen Brown

BUILD OUR KINGDOM PUBLISHING
—— BUILD OUR KINGDOM ——

Escape The Rat Race God's Way

Copyright © 2024 by Build Our Kingdom Publishing, LLC and Allen Brown

Published by Build Our Kingdom Publishing, LLC

All rights reserved. This book or any portion thereof may not be reproduced or used in any manner whatsoever without the express written permission of the publisher except for the use of brief quotations in a book review.

Printed in the United States of America
1st Edition March 2024 First Printing

ISBN for paperback: 978-1-7350588-7-0
Build Our Kingdom Publishing, LLC. 560 Main St, Stroudsburg, PA 18360
www.BuildOurKingdom.com
Scripture taken from the New King James Version®. Copyright © 1982 by Thomas Nelson. Used by permission. All rights reserved.

Scripture quotations marked (NIV) are taken from the Holy Bible, New International Version®, NIV®. Copyright © 1973, 19 78, 1984, 2011 by Biblica, Inc.™ Used by permission of Zondervan. All rights reserved worldwide. www.zondervan.com The "NIV" and "New International Version" are trademarks registered in the United States Patent and Trademark Office by Biblica, Inc™

Although the publisher and the author have made every effort to ensure that the information in this book was correct at press time and while this publication is designed to provide accurate information in regard to the subject matter covered, the publisher and the author assume no responsibility for errors, inaccuracies, omissions, or any other inconsistencies herein and hereby disclaim any liability to any party for any loss, damage, or disruption caused by errors or omissions, whether such errors or omissions result from negligence, accident, or any other cause.

This publication is meant as a source of valuable information for the reader, however, it is not meant as a substitute for direct expert assistance. If such a level of assistance is required, the services of a competent professional should be sought.

Table of Content

Letter From Pastor Allen Brown v

Opening Prayer vii

INTRODUCTION Escaping the Rat Race God's Way 1

Chapter 1 The Wealth in Jesus Earthly Ministry 13

Chapter 2 Your Supernatural Blessings Await! 25

Chapter 3 Canceling Your Debts and Building Wealth 47

Chapter 4 Multiplication and Leveraging Resources 71

Chapter 5 The Wisdom of Mentorship 95

Chapter 6 Your Faithful Journey to Financial Freedom 123

Chapter 7 Your Seed Can Change Your Life 135

Closing Prayer 156

About the Author 159

LETTER FROM PASTOR ALLEN BROWN

Dear Believer,

Embarking on a journey toward financial independence and prosperity under God's guidance is not just a path but a divine invitation to align with Kingdom principles. This book is a testament to the transformative power of faith and obedience, drawing from firsthand experiences and biblical wisdom that have shaped my journey from a young entrepreneur to a successful business owner, real estate investor, and steward of a thriving ministry.

From the age of eighteen, when I signed my first official business lease, to owning a commercial building with 11 units, my journey has been marked by a steadfast faith in God's provisions and the application of Kingdom economics. These experiences are not shared to boast but to offer insight into the possibilities that unfold when we align our financial endeavors with divine principles.

This book aims to shed light on the path to financial freedom, guided by the lessons learned through successes and divine guidance. It's a blueprint for those seeking to escape the rat race, not through conventional wisdom, but through the application of biblical truths that promise prosperity and abundance.

Your support of this ministry, whether through prayer, engagement, or financial contribution, is invaluable. It's a partnership in faith, advancing the Kingdom's work and enabling us to share God's blessings more broadly. As you delve into these pages, I invite you to open your heart to the lessons within, ready to embark on a transformative journey toward achieving the financial freedom you desire, under God's watchful guidance.

Should you feel moved to connect or seek further guidance, know that I am here, ready to assist and pray for you. Together, let's explore how divine principles can illuminate our paths, leading us to a life of abundance and fulfillment, as intended by our Creator.

Pastor Allen Brown

OPENING PRAYER FOR GUIDANCE AND BLESSING ON YOUR JOURNEY

Dear Heavenly Father,

As I embark on the journey within these pages, I pause to lift my heart and mind to You, seeking Your divine guidance and blessing. You are the source of all wisdom, understanding, and knowledge, and I acknowledge my need for Your insight as I navigate the paths laid out before me.

Lord, bless this book and me as I read it. May it serve as a vessel through which Your truth, light, and love are communicated to me. Open my eyes to the lessons You have for me and prepare my heart to receive and apply these truths in my life.

Grant me the courage to explore the depths of Your wisdom shared here. Let each word be a seed planted in fertile soil within me, growing and flourishing under Your watchful care. May this book not just be a collection of pages, but a journey of transformation for me, bringing me closer to Your heart and Your plans for my life.

I pray for inspiration and clarity as I seek to learn from this work. May my life be enriched, my faith strengthened, and my steps directed more firmly on the path You have set before me. Let this book be a source of encouragement, a beacon of hope, and a reflection of Your infinite love.

In all things, I give You the glory and honor.
In Jesus' precious name
Amen

INTRODUCTION

ESCAPING THE RAT RACE GOD'S WAY

This resource is designed to help you gain understanding and insight into how the Bible, centuries ago, laid out principles for achieving financial freedom. Many people, particularly in America and other predominantly Christian societies, have overlooked these biblical teachings. As a result, they have been misled into believing that the systems of this world are the only way to operate. This mindset prevents them from seeing how God can bless and multiply their efforts, generating wealth and creating self-sustaining financial avenues.

This book will share practical ways to operate, offering processes for wealth generation the biblical way. It's important to understand that being caught in the "rat race" was never meant to be your future. If you are unfamiliar with the term "rat race," it refers to a frustrating, hard-to-break cycle where individuals work primarily to pay bills without making significant financial progress or achieving personal satisfaction.

If you find yourself working merely to survive, without having set up any mechanisms in your life to leverage your time, then this book is for you.

The Bible is a treasure trove of ancient wisdom that has guided many throughout history. However, some people believe that God desires only worship, without providing believers a way to generate wealth or sustain their daily lives. This is a misconception. God seeks a personal relationship with you and wants to partner with you on earth. Indeed, the Bible mentions this partnership, especially in Romans 8:17, where it discusses believers being "heirs of God and co-heirs with Christ." This partnership isn't limited to spiritual matters or religious practices; it extends to helping you make progress in life and, in return, enabling you to bless others in various ways.

Helping others can take many forms, from offering physical assistance to sharing knowledge and insights. However, the ability to provide significant help often requires financial resources. For instance, offering someone temporary shelter today means having a place for which you are financially responsible.

It's not commonly discussed, but Jesus' ministry was supported by financial contributions. This is evidenced in the Gospel of John 12:6, where Judas Iscariot is mentioned as the treasurer, who managed the money bag for Jesus and His disciples. This aspect of Jesus' life highlights the importance of finances in sustaining ministry and service efforts.

With this context, this book aims to introduce biblical principles that guide wealth accumulation. It reassures you that seeking wealth is not inherently wrong, but we should remain humble in the process as its God that gives us the ability to do so as highlighted in the following scriptures. **Deuteronomy 8:18**, states, **"But remember the Lord your God, for it is he who gives you the ability to produce wealth."** Similarly, **Ecclesiastes 5:19** mentions, **"Moreover, when God gives someone wealth and possessions, and the ability to enjoy them, to accept their lot and be happy in their toil—this is a gift of God."** God is not against wealth building, but these scriptures are presented so we remain humble in our pursuit of it.

By sharing these principles, this guide seeks to help you break free from the rat race, empowering you to achieve financial freedom and live a life of purpose and abundance, as envisioned in the Bible.

What I'm going to do in this book is take several scriptures and break down some scriptural insights that you can look at and analyze, and then, as soon as possible, start implementing them in your life. It's the reason why they're here. They're supposed to be a guiding light to the transformation from where we are to where we can go by taking biblical concepts and applying them in our life as soon as possible.

The reason why we shouldn't delay is because the more time you take to implement, the longer it takes for you to find success. It is particularly important that you fail really fast because the faster you learn from your failures, the more you can improve on your journey. This is not something you want to do when you don't have the energy or the ability to put in the time and work. This is something you want to do when you can actually dedicate your time and efforts to making something out of what

God has already put inside of you before you even entered the Earth realm.

7 Key Principles Highlighted in This Book

The Bible is loaded with principles and laws designed to guide us towards achieving various successes in life. Among these, I will focus on seven pivotal principles as we navigate through each chapter of this book, highlighting when and how these principles come into play.

1. Faith

The cornerstone principle is faith. As stated in the Book of Hebrews, it is impossible to please God without faith. **"But without faith it is impossible to please him: for he that cometh to God must believe that he is, and that he is a rewarder of them that diligently seek him." (Hebrews 11:6)** Operating in faith is foundational in pleasing our Lord, and while faith comes in many measures, even a small amount can be the seed from which greater things grow. This book will explore how starting with a small act of faith can lead to significant achievements.

2. OBEDIENCE

Before one can receive anything from God, obedience is crucial. Many spend their time conforming to worldly expectations, which often contradict divine instructions. This book will share stories of how obedience has led to rewards, including my own experiences, emphasizing the importance of taking God at His word and following His guidance to reach desired destinations.

3. SACRIFICE

Sacrifice is key to transforming your life because it may require you to forgo or relinquish something to access God's supernatural interventions. **"And he said to them all, if any man will come after me, let him deny himself, and take up his cross daily, and follow me." (Luke 9:23)** God's principles work universally, as He is not a respecter of persons but of principles. Adhering to these principles opens doors to blessings, as outlined in Galatians 6: **"Be not deceived; God is not mocked: for whatsoever a man soweth, that shall he also reap." (Galatians 6:7)**

4. WISDOM

Wisdom, which is the application of knowledge, is paramount. **"Wisdom is the principal thing; therefore get wisdom: and with all thy getting get understanding." (Proverbs 4:7)** The Bible asserts that in all your acquiring, prioritize wisdom and understanding. This book will demonstrate how applying wisdom, the practical use of knowledge, can lead to the outcomes God intends for us.

5. RESOURCEFULNESS

Understanding that God's provision often exceeds our expectations encourages a mindset of resourcefulness. Recognizing the potential in what God provides, like seeing a seed rather than just a tree, can lead to growth and multiplication beyond what we initially pray for. This principle teaches us to see and utilize God's gifts and the small things in life effectively. Remember, God can take limited resources and multiply it for you.

6. GRATITUDE

Maintaining gratitude through every season, whether challenging or prosperous, acknowledges God's sovereignty over our circumstances. This book will discuss how embracing gratitude, especially during trials, cultivates patience and endurance necessary for the blessings ahead.

7. GENEROSITY

The final principle focuses on generosity, a virtue that God greatly honors. The measure and intent of your giving can unlock divine returns. This book will illustrate how generosity, even when it challenges our faith or requires sacrifice, opens spiritual doors that lead to abundant blessings in alignment with God's promises.

THE VALUE YOU BRING TO THE WORLD

Transitioning from spiritual principles, I will discuss the marketplace and personal development, where value creation is critical. Reflecting on Jesus' ministry and the magnetic value He offered, this section parallels how offering significant value in today's marketplace can attract success and fulfillment.

7 Core Attributes of Value That Will Help You in Your Journey to Wealth

1. Reliability speaks to your consistency and dependability, reassuring others of your steadfastness in both professional and personal settings. This quality is fundamental in building trust, as it shows you are reliable and can be counted on to deliver what you promise, whether it be a product, a service, or a personal commitment. Being seen as dependable strengthens relationships with customers and loved ones alike, fostering a sense of security and mutual respect.

2. Innovation reflects your commitment to progress and improvement, making your offerings continually appealing and your personal growth constant. It signals to others that you are forward-thinking and always looking for ways to enhance your products, services, or self. This drive for innovation encourages a dynamic approach to problem-solving and creativity, making you a valued partner in business and a stimulating companion in life.

3. Empathy underscores your ability to connect and resonate with others on a personal level, making them feel understood and valued. This connection is crucial for building strong, meaningful relationships, whether with your audience, customers, or in your personal circles. Empathy enhances your ability to communicate effectively and forge deep connections, proving essential in both professional collaborations and personal relationships.

4. Passion is the driving force that showcases your genuine enthusiasm and belief in what you do, attracting others to your cause. This fervor is not only infectious but also deeply inspiring, significantly influencing how people perceive you and your work. A passionate individual not only excels in their professional endeavors but also brings vitality and inspiration into their personal interactions.

5. Flexibility demonstrates your adaptability to change and challenges, proving your dedication to meeting others' needs in the marketplace and in personal situations. This quality shows you are agile and can pivot as necessary to address the evolving demands of your industry, customers, or the dynamic nature of personal life. Flexibility is a testament to your resilience and commitment to maintaining relationships and professional standing, even under pressure.

6. Transparency is about being open and honest in your dealings, providing clarity around your business practices, pricing, and the benefits and limitations of your products or services, as well as in your intentions and actions in personal interactions. This openness fosters trust and reassures those around you, both customers and personal acquaintances, that they can make informed decisions and have genuine relationships.

7. Commitment to Quality ensures that every product, service, or personal action you offer meets a high standard of quality, reassuring those around you that they are engaging with someone who values excellence. A commitment to quality sets you apart from competitors in business and elevates your personal interactions, leading to positive recognition, word-of-mouth, and the strengthening of both professional and personal bonds.

By embodying these seven attributes—reliability, innovation, empathy, passion, flexibility, transparency, and a commitment to quality—you solidify the value you bring to the table. Each trait plays a vital role in establishing your worth, both in the marketplace and in the lives of those you impact personally.

As we close this introduction, we've only just begun to scratch the surface of achieving success by aligning with God's principles. Chapter 1 promises to guide you further, offering wisdom and insights tailored for those eager to escape the rat race, God's way. Let's step forward together, ready to embrace the principles that will light your path to a life of fulfillment and true achievement.

CHAPTER 1

THE WEALTH IN JESUS EARTHLY MINISTRY

In this book, I'm going to explore various different areas of the Bible, presenting stories that shed light on aspects often overlooked by many Christians. Some of the insights we'll discuss may challenge your existing perceptions of religion, God, and spirituality. One crucial point I want to make clear from the outset is that living in poverty or lack is not God's desire for you. The Bible speaks of abundance, and achieving this abundance first requires a shift in mindset about wealth and prosperity.

THE REVELATION OF FINANCIAL STEWARDSHIP IN JESUS' MINISTRY

Our first revelation comes from a closer examination of Judas Iscariot's role as the treasurer for Jesus Christ, which is a testament to Christ not being a beggar but rather rich in resources due to the support his ministry received. John 12:6 highlights Judas' objection to Mary's use of expensive perfume on Jesus, not out of concern for the poor but because he was stealing from the money bag. This incident alone prompts us to consider the financial dynamics within Jesus' ministry more deeply.

Going back to verse 5, we encounter Judas questioning why the perfume wasn't sold to benefit the poor, estimating its value at a year's wages. This detail is pivotal as it not only reveals Judas' ulterior motives but also underscores the presence of valuable assets within Jesus' ministry. The fact that such an expensive item, worth a year's wages, was readily available and not a cause for concern highlights the level of wealth and resources at their disposal. This point challenges the common misconception of Jesus living in poverty. Instead, it illustrates that His ministry was characterized by abundance, capable of handling valuable assets without worry. This revelation is crucial for changing the mindset that equates spiritual righteousness with material poverty, suggesting that wealth and spiritual fulfillment can coexist. Think about that!

Many believers overlook such details, adhering to a notion of false humility that equates lack with holiness. However, this perspective is far from the truth. God does not glorify in our poverty but rather in our ability to manage and utilize resources wisely. The passage from John 12:1-6 reveals that Jesus' ministry had access to significant assets, challenging the misconception that Jesus and his followers lived in destitution.

LEVERAGING RESOURCES FOR MINISTRY

This brings us to an essential secret revealed through Scripture: the misconception that we must labor in conventional ways without leveraging our resources is flawed. The presence of expensive perfume, and the suggestion that it could be sold, indicates that Jesus' ministry engaged in commerce to some extent to support its activities. There's no evidence that Jesus ever had to pause his ministry to earn wages in a conventional manner, suggesting a model of resource management and financial independence that allowed for continuous ministry and movement.

Asking "What would Jesus do?" (WWJD) in this context urges us to reconsider our approach to financial stewardship and resource utilization. If Jesus had resources at his disposal, why shouldn't we also seek to manage our resources wisely and sustain our ministries, business or personal missions?

MORE INSIGHT ABOUT JESUS

In examining Luke 8:1-3, we unearth a pivotal dimension of Jesus' ministry, shining a light on the mechanisms of support and contribution that underpinned His mission. This passage, while seemingly straightforward, harbors profound insights into the economics of value exchange and support systems that sustained Jesus' work. It's a testament to a model of financial independence that's both enlightening and instructive for us today.

THE VALUE OF PREPARATION AND SPECIALIZATION

A vital takeaway from Jesus' journey is the sheer importance of preparation and honing one's skills. Reflect on the narrative of Jesus at the age of 12, engaging with religious leaders in the temple (Luke 2:42-49). This wasn't merely a display of precociousness but a glimpse into the years of learning and preparation that Jesus undertook long before His public ministry began. Like Jesus, who was already absorbing, learning, and preparing for His future role from such a young age, we too must dedicate ourselves to mastering our crafts. The more specialized and skilled you become in your chosen field, the more value you can offer, positioning yourself for financial abundance. This is not about being jack-of-all-trades but mastering specific skills that set you apart.

THE ECONOMICS OF VALUE EXCHANGE

Focusing on the latter part of Luke 8:1-3, we see a direct correlation between the value Jesus provided and the support He received. Notably, women like Mary Magdalene, from whom seven demons were cast out, and Joanna, the wife of Chuza, the manager of Herod's household, were transformed by Jesus' ministry, leading them to support His mission from their resources. This wasn't merely charity but a response to the significant value Jesus had added to their lives by liberating them from afflictions and providing them with profound spiritual and physical healing. The lesson here is clear: the value you bring to others can translate into financial support for your endeavors. It's about creating a cycle of value and reciprocation that benefits all parties involved.

Value Tip

Your ability to add value to others' lives can lead to meaningful support for your endeavors. Cultivate a culture of reciprocity by consistently delivering value.

THE PRINCIPLE OF SUSTAINED VALUE

Jesus' ministry exemplifies the creation of sustained value. His healing and teachings weren't one-off transactions; they were life-changing interventions that continued to resonate with individuals long after the initial encounter. This approach to creating lasting impact is something I've mirrored in my own ventures, such as the music platform I developed in 2005 called rocbattle.com. This platform wasn't just a business; it was a means to provide ongoing value to music producers. By setting up a system that continuously serves users, I created a model where a one-time effort results in recurring revenue. This mirrors the biblical principle of sowing seeds that yield ongoing harvests.

IMPLEMENTING BIBLICAL PRINCIPLES IN MODERN VENTURES

Drawing from personal experience, the music platform I mentioned served as a case study in applying these biblical principles. I built this system once, but it continued to provide value to music producers and it helped them grow in their skills, ensuring a steady stream of income. This is the essence of what Jesus achieved through His healing and teachings. He offered something of lasting value—be it liberation from demons or profound spiritual insights—that compelled those He helped to support His ministry continually.

CONCLUSION: THE POWER OF SERVICE AND VALUE

The narrative in Luke 8:1-3 is more than historical recounting; it's a blueprint for transcending traditional economic constraints through the principles of preparation, specialization, and sustained value creation. By genuinely serving others and providing significant value, we not only fulfill our higher calling but also lay the groundwork for financial prosperity that mirrors the biblical model of support and abundance.

As we go deeper into these teachings, we're invited to reconsider our approaches to wealth, service, and value creation. It challenges us to question: how quickly can we adapt these life-altering principles, leveraging our talents to serve others while building a sustainable foundation and wealth for our future?

REFLECTION AND IMPLEMENTATION

As we reach the end of this chapter, it's crucial to not only absorb the insights shared but also to reflect on how you can apply these principles in your own life. Below are some guided questions and exercises designed to help you translate theory into action. Take a moment to ponder these questions, and jot down your responses. This exercise is not just about self-discovery but about laying the groundwork for tangible change.

IDENTIFY YOUR VALUE

Discover Your Strengths: What are the skills or activities you excel in that could bring value to others? List these things, focusing on those you feel passionate about and that others have noticed.

_____

_____

_____

_____

_____

_____

_____

_____

_____

_____

_____

_____

_____

_____

Recognize Underestimated Talents: Reflect on the feedback you've received over the years. What skills have others praised that you've downplayed? Could these talents potentially generate income through a service or product? Write down these insights.

_____

_____

_____

_____

_____

_____

_____

_____

_____

_____

_____

_____

_____

_____

_____

Conceptualize Your Offerings: How can you transform your skills and knowledge into products or services? Whether it's writing a book, offering consulting services, or creating a unique product, think about mediums through which your talents can shine and generate monetary value. List your ideas here.

_____

_____

_____

_____

_____

_____

_____

_____

_____

_____

_____

_____

_____

_____

KEY CONCEPTS REVIEW FOR CHAPTER 1

To ensure you've grasped the core principles of this chapter, let's recap the key concepts discussed:

Leverage: The importance of using available resources to your advantage, maximizing the impact of your efforts.

Value Creation: The focus on providing significant value to others, which in turn can lead to financial prosperity.

Money Management: Understanding and implementing effective strategies for managing the financial support or income generated through your endeavors.

Resourcefulness: The ability to creatively use your skills, knowledge, and connections to overcome obstacles and generate wealth.

CHAPTER 2

YOUR SUPERNATURAL BLESSINGS AWAIT!

There was much to gather from the previous chapter, particularly regarding the value Jesus contributed to sustain His ministry. We observed that those who supported Him remained steadfast, a testament to the ongoing exchange of services and value.

As we explore more into this narrative, setting the stage for understanding Jesus' successful ministry surrounded by financial resources, it's crucial to recognize the existence of the supernatural. By 'supernatural,' I refer to a state beyond our natural existence, encompassing phenomena that often defy explanation due to divine intervention entering our lives when we believe. The key concept here revolves around our belief.

For believers in Christ, it's essential to understand the unique advantage we possess. With Christ as our advocate and friend, partnering with Him offers benefits unattainable to the secular world, enabling supernatural shifts in our circumstances. However, the only barrier to receiving these supernatural blessings is our belief system—believing that we must acquire things as the world does limit our potential. Engaging with Jesus Christ and expecting outcomes beyond the norm invites into our life's unexplainable timings and events capable of altering our destiny. The prerequisite for such a transformation is belief in the possibility of these occurrences.

As we progress through this book, I'll share several personal experiences of supernatural events that have radically changed my perspective, moving beyond conventional thought processes. The world's approach to financial gain does not align with what I term 'Kingdom economics.'

Scripture advises us to **"seek ye first the kingdom of God, and He will add everything unto you." Matthew 6:33** Being part of the kingdom and understanding its principles, which I call Kingdom economics, necessitates a shift in expectation from that of non-believers. Unfortunately, many spend years unaware of Kingdom economics, even within the Christian community, leading to a life of mediocrity and a hopeless quest for miracles, all the while succumbing to the world's rat race.

I aim to demonstrate that altering your mindset requires faith and the courage to undertake actions you've never considered before. In the following paragraphs, I will share my personal journey alongside key biblical principles, equipping you with the knowledge needed to break free from the rat race and thrive within the Kingdom economy.

THE WIDOW'S OFFERING LEADING TO ELIJAH'S PROVISION (1 KINGS 17:8-16)

This is one of the first stories I'm going to share in this book, outside of Jesus Christ, which presents to us a spiritual process. This process represents acting in faith, being obedient, and receiving returns on what you give. Before I break this down, I want to share that many people, even believers, do not accept the stories in the Bible as real and something that can happen to them. This level of skepticism or even doubt pushes you away from God. To witness the rewards of the supernatural and the blessings that God can bring, which result in abundance, you have to step outside of anything that was taught to you, try God, and test Him to see that what He presented in the Bible can very well happen in your life. The problem is most people don't have enough faith to actually wholeheartedly trust the Lord on this side of Heaven. The mindset is if I cannot tangibly think of what the results can be, I'm not going to act in any type of faith until I have assurance that I'm going to get a return. My friend, if you think like this, you will never receive the abundance and the supernatural from God.

I want to focus on the scripture and right after, share a very important testimony from my life. The following scripture that I'm going to break down goes into Elijah's provisions when trusting and following God.

"8 Then the word of the Lord came to him: 9 'Go at once to Zarephath in the region of Sidon and stay there. I have directed a widow there to supply you with food.'" We see that the Lord gave a specific instruction. What you must realize is that God, if you yield to Him and be sensitive to His Spirit, can give you instructions. This is not just for the days of Bible characters. If you clear the noise in your life and dedicate time to commune with God, God will speak directly to you in different ways. Sometimes He will speak directly to your heart, sometimes through other people, and sometimes through different events and situations. But once you get to know God more, you'll be able to identify when He is speaking to you. So, what Elijah does here is he follows the instructions and does exactly what the Lord instructed him to do.

In part of receiving your supernatural blessings, you have to understand that God has people already in position to bless you. You will never know this until you step out on faith, but once you do and see it happen, your faith will increase to know that God will always provide for you. You just have to be obedient and listen to the instructions that He gives, and He will handle the rest. We learn here in verse 9 that He said He had already given direction for a widow to supply food for him.

Now at this point, some believers will not proceed because they will have too much skepticism. What if I get there and the woman doesn't feed me? Or what if I get there and they don't answer the door? Or what if I get there and they just reject me? When God gives you instructions, you have to follow them, even if all the above happens and you don't see it work out right away. The rejections and blocked doors often put you right in the place you are supposed to be. Even when you don't see what God is saying or your results are not coming yet, you have to trust and believe with super expectations that God is not going to fail you once He tells you what He's going to do. Just continue to follow His instruction.

"10 So he went to Zarephath. When he came to the town gate, a widow was there gathering sticks. He called to her and asked, 'Would you bring me a little water in a jar so I may have a drink?'" Verse 10 shares with us that Elijah went, as the Bible says, so he went. When God tells you to go somewhere, make sure you go. The Bible then says he came into a town, and a widow was gathering sticks. He called and asked, "Hey, may I get something to drink?" This was not a problem for the widow woman, and she responded by going to get him what he had asked for.

"11 As she was going to get it, he called, 'And bring me, please, a piece of bread.' 12 'As surely as the Lord your God lives,' she replied, 'I don't have any bread—only a handful of flour in a jar and a little olive

oil in a jug. I am gathering a few sticks to take home and make a meal for myself and my son, that we may eat it—and die.'" As the woman was going to get it, he called out and asked if she could bring him some bread. Her response was that she didn't have any bread and then began to explain to him the limited amount of stuff that she had. She then explained to him her real-life situation of lack by stating she was gathering a few sticks to take home and make a meal for herself and her son, that they may eat something and die.

What we learn here is that the widow woman herself was in a dire situation. If you ask me, she probably had a mindset which would keep her repeating the same process of living in lack, or what we might call in this book, being in the rat race. There's a high majority of people that live amongst us that are only one paycheck away from being kicked out or removed from the little bit of comfort that they have. And the reality is it doesn't have to be this way. Just learning a little bit and applying a bit of principles supplied by God can change lives all around. But somehow, as Christians, we are not shaped in our minds to give our last to move forward. Many Christians miss the principle of giving, and because they are always trying to get, they miss the sacrificial process of growing in abundance and totally misguide principles for their life to have wealth and prosperity.

"13 Elijah said to her, 'Don't be afraid. Go home and do as you have said. But first make a small loaf of bread for me from what you have and bring it to me, and then make something for yourself and your son.'" This verse would lose 95% of God's children in the Kingdom. The reason why I say this is because if someone told you when you were on your last to give to them first, it would not make any logical sense because you would feel the need to sustain yourself before you even chose to give to someone else. This is how the world works, but in the Kingdom, where faith is required to move and bring abundance, you would fail if you operated like this in this particular situation. God would not move on your behalf. The reason would be because you didn't exercise in faith, and God in His word says that it is impossible to please Him unless you have faith and that He is a rewarder of those who diligently seek Him. The process of diligently seeking Him is seeking His wisdom, His knowledge, and understanding because when you seek all of that information, you then now operate in the principles and the mind of God to receive the blessings that He so promises in His word.

"14 For this is what the Lord, the God of Israel, says: 'The jar of flour will not be used up and the jug of oil will not run dry until the day the Lord sends rain on the land.'" In verse 14, we see the prophet share with the woman a prophetic word, basically telling her what God had inspired him to say to her and instruct her to do, and the promise that will come as a result. This is the point where you have to believe. When I think about my now spiritual logic, which I have grown into, there's absolutely no way I would not listen to what the prophet shared with me. Think about it. What do I have to lose? It's my last anyway. The best thing for me to do is activate the spiritual principle of giving and make a sacrificial gesture to give my last.

Most Christians don't understand the power in being in this position of lack and not having anything. God looks at your giving as sacrificial because even though what you give, someone else could give in abundance, it wouldn't be their last. God looks at it as you are exercising faith because it's all you have, and you are trusting that He will come through on His promise. That process is what you can do right now. Even in the worst situations you can look for something you can give. This principle activates your harvest. I would challenge you to look at your last to get your next blessing and watch what God does. You can't have scary faith an expect God to do the impossible.

"15 She went away and did as Elijah had told her. So there was food every day for Elijah and for the woman and her family. 16 For the jar of flour was not used up and the jug of oil did not run dry, in keeping with the word of the Lord spoken by Elijah." This passage illustrates the woman's immediate compliance with Elijah's instructions. Notably, the Bible does not mention any objections from her, highlighting a remarkable event. Despite her limited resources, the Bible records that there was food daily for Elijah, the woman, and her family. This exemplifies the power of faith and the importance of adhering to God's directives.

God possesses knowledge far beyond our understanding. By positioning us precisely where we need to be, He ensures the right people enter our lives to meet our needs, thus eliminating much of the guesswork. Relying on God to perform the supernatural allows us to focus on utilizing our gifts and talents, trusting in Him to do the rest.

A critical caution to heed when applying God's principles is to avoid diluting them with personal ideologies or secular reasoning, as this can hinder your blessings. Attempting to supplement God's work with human logic only disrupts the flow of His blessings. If God instructs you to speak with someone, do so without hesitation, even if the outcome appears uncertain initially. Trust in God's plan. Similarly, if directed to a specific place, questioning the location is unnecessary.

There may be times when you seek confirmation, and God will reaffirm His instructions if they were not clear or understood initially. Do not hesitate to request clarity from God; you might be surprised to hear Him repeat His guidance in many ways. However, the key is to follow His directions, regardless of how much they may challenge conventional wisdom.

God's logic transcends worldly reasoning, aligning with His spiritual order that governs His Kingdom. This divine logic positions us perfectly within the realm of kingdom economics, necessary for our prosperity on Earth. As observed in the concluding verse, the jar of flour and the oil jug remained full, consistent with God's promise and Elijah's prophecy to the woman, displaying God's unwavering faithfulness and provision.

THE SAME PRINCIPLE IN MY LIFE

Let me share with you briefly how these same principles we just went over actually happen in my life. It was at a time when I was tired of working as a barber, even though I was making good money. I was just working to maintain the things that I had—my home, my car, my businesses, and stuff of that nature—the regular stuff that any middle-class family would have and maintain. What I did not have was the freedom that I needed to spend time with my then young family. Therefore, I prayed to God and asked Him, "God, could you give me time to spend with my family?" And the response that I got from God was just to walk away from everything, give everything away, sell everything, and then you will have what you want. I thought this was the craziest thing in the world as a new Christian, and I did not respond to it right away. So, within the next 6 months, I continued feeling the same way I did, and I went to God and prayed about it again. Well, let me share with you that God didn't change His mind. He told me the same thing: give everything away, and I will take care of you. This time, I listened, and because I listened, everything changed.

I'll give you the abbreviated story, but I wrote this entire story down in my book, ***"Million Dollar Seed. How My Last $17,600 Grew to Millions God's Way."*** In that book, I document from when God told me to give everything away to when I finally got down to my last bit of money and I prayed to God and asked Him how come He didn't bless me like He said He would. Come to find out, I was supposed to give my last $17,600 away, and I was holding on to it after I already gave over $100,000 in material possessions and money away. I thought that I could hold on to my last bit of money because I had already given away so much, which included my home, cars, furniture, and money. What God shared with me in my last prayer before my breakthrough was, "You gave all these things away, but I told you to give everything away, and you still held on to $17,600." Well, I cannot share with you all the details that are written in the book here, but I will tell you this. I gave my last $17,600 to a random pastor who I didn't know. God led me to a woman pastor names Bishop Eva Stinson and instructed me to give my last money to her. After I put the money in the pastor's hand, I came to find out that her son, whom I didn't know personally but knew of his name, was a famous producer in the music business named "Rockwilder." Rockwilder at the time was behind 70 million record sales and had won two Grammy Awards. Long story short, the pastor introduced me to her son, and within a short period of time after we started a business that generated millions. The name of the business was rocbattle.com which we launched in 2005-06. That business registered thousands of producers and was successful for years. The result was I was able to have free time with my family, which was exactly what I prayed for. This allowed me to live like I was retired and gave me leveraged income that was coming to me month to month from members' subscriptions and music production sales.

I know the Bible presents a lot of stories, and sometimes we might have a hard time thinking that these things could happen in our life. But until you step out in faith and ask God for the changes you want, and then follow His instructions, you'll never live like the Bible characters. You will just be a mediocre Christian living in a world using worldly concepts and systems to survive. Which it all cancels out what God can do for you in the supernatural. I will never go back to living in worldly concepts, as the Bible says, **"Do not conform to the pattern of this world, but be transformed by the renewing of your mind. Then you will be able to test and approve what God's will is—his good, pleasing and perfect will." Romans 12:2**

If you want to see yourself get out of the Rat Race and receive supernatural blessings from God, it's going to take you exercising faith and believing in God through the process that He has specifically designed for you. Everyone is different, and what God will call you to do may be different, but the principles remain the same: sacrificial giving and making sacrifices when God instructs is key. It will actually reproduce favor over your life, sustaining you for years to come.

When I decided to do what I did, that was in 2004. In 2005, that business was launched, and currently, as of the writing of this book in February 2024, that sacrificial gift that I gave to that pastor is still paying me in multiple ways to this date. I currently have a site called buybeats.com that is thriving. That website is a direct result of the blessings that came with my site rocbattle.com.

Rockwilder and Allen Brown. Rocbattle.com photo shoot 2006

Reflection and Application for Chapter 2

As we conclude Chapter 2, focusing on understanding the supernatural in your financial life through biblical examples, it's essential not only to reflect on these stories but also to consider how their principles can be applied in your own life. Below are some guided questions and exercises designed to help you translate the lessons of faith, obedience, and supernatural provision into actionable steps. Take a moment to ponder these questions, and jot down your responses to facilitate a deeper understanding and application of these principles.

IDENTIFY OPPORTUNITIES FOR FAITH-BASED ACTION

Reflect on Your Own 'Zarephath': What is your current 'Zarephath' situation where you need to step out in faith? Think about a scenario in your life that requires you to trust in God's provision despite the odds. Write down the steps you can take to demonstrate your faith.

_____
_____
_____
_____
_____
_____
_____
_____
_____
_____
_____
_____
_____

Recognize Your 'Widow's Offering': Reflect on what you have that you can offer in faith, even if it seems small or insignificant. How can this act of giving lead to a supernatural return? List any resources, talents, or time you can offer as your 'widow's mite.'

KEY CONCEPTS REVIEW

To ensure you've internalized the core lessons from this chapter, let's recap the key concepts discussed:

Supernatural Provision: The belief that God can provide for our needs in miraculous ways, beyond our human understanding or efforts.

Acting in Faith: The necessity of stepping out in faith, especially when God's instructions seem counterintuitive or challenging.

Obedience to Divine Instructions: Understanding that obedience to God's specific directions is often a prerequisite for receiving His blessings.

Sacrificial Giving: Recognizing the power and importance of giving from our scarcity, trusting that God will honor our faithfulness with abundance.

FAITH ACTION PLAN:

Create a plan detailing how you intend to apply a step of faith in a specific area of your life. Include what you will give, how you plan to step out in faith, and the spiritual principles you're relying on.

_____
_____
_____
_____
_____
_____
_____
_____
_____
_____
_____
_____
_____
_____
_____

REFLECTION

This chapter has aimed to deepen your understanding of the supernatural aspects of God's provision and how acting in faith, following divine instructions, and giving sacrificially can lead to miraculous outcomes in our lives. As you reflect on these stories and principles, consider the steps you can take to incorporate this level of trust and obedience into your financial stewardship and daily living.

CHAPTER 3

CANCELING YOUR DEBTS AND BUILDING WEALTH

Another notable widow in the Bible is found in 2 Kings Chapter 4. This time, it's not Elijah, but Elisha who encounters a widow in need and reaches out to the prophet. This widow is in debt and facing the loss of her two sons to slavery if she doesn't cover this debt. The situation stems from her husband having died, leaving her to fend for herself.

No one is exempt from landing on hard times. This can be any of us at any given time, as we can face different situations that change all the financial dynamics around us. We can never say never, but more importantly, it's about the process to move out of these situations and possibly operating in a system that prevents us from getting into it anymore.

What we must observe in this particular situation is that the husband took care of everything, and possibly, this wife was unaware of how to sustain the family with regard to income and finances. Left alone, she fell on hard times, not having the information or awareness to continue. Let's take a deeper look into this situation.

THE WIDOW'S OIL MULTIPLIED (2 KINGS 4:1-7)

4:1 "The wife of a man from the company of the prophets cried out to Elisha, 'Your servant, my husband, is dead, and you know that he revered the Lord. But now his creditor is coming to take my two boys as his slaves.'"

One of the first things she does is explain the situation to Elisha. Her husband was part of the company of prophets and had passed away. She explains to Elisha that he revered the Lord. But now, she's facing a situation with creditors that could result in her sons becoming slaves to pay off the debt. Even though, in today's time, in our current society, you may not become a physical slave. However, if you structure your life to be obligated beyond what you can handle, you can very much turn yourself into a slave, trying to repay creditors or, worse, lose possessions as a result of the debts you owe.

UNDERSTANDING THE VALUE WITHIN

2 "Elisha replied to her, 'How can I help you? Tell me, what do you have in your house?' 'Your servant has nothing there at all,' she said, 'except a small jar of olive oil.'"

In this question from Elisha, we uncover a significant lesson on awareness and self-assessment in the face of adversity. Elisha's inquiry into what the widow already possesses within her home challenges us to reconsider our own perceptions of scarcity and potential. This moment illuminates a common oversight among many: the failure to recognize the value and resources we hold. The widow's initial response, "Your servant has nothing at all," mirrors a widespread mindset that undervalues what is readily available to us, focusing on what we lack rather than what we have.

This narrative prompts a deeper reflection on how we identify and utilize our resources, skills, talents, money, etc. The widow's realization that she possesses a small jar of olive oil, although seemingly insignificant, symbolizes the untapped potential within each of us. It's a call to shift our perspective from one of deficiency to one of possibility, recognizing that solutions to our challenges may already lie within our grasp.

Elisha's guidance to the widow serves as an encouragement to look beyond the surface, urging us to seek spiritual insight and revelation in our circumstances. It suggests that many of us possess the tools necessary to navigate our difficulties and achieve our goals, yet we may be unaware of them due to a limited perspective.

Through this question, we are reminded of the importance of taking stock of our resources, no matter how small or inconsequential they may seem. It teaches us to engage in a deeper exploration of our abilities and assets, encouraging a mindset of resourcefulness and faith. It's not just about recognizing what we have but also about the transformative power of acting upon this recognition under divine guidance.

ACTING ON ELISHA'S INSTRUCTIONS

3 "Elisha said, 'Go around and ask all your neighbors for empty jars. Don't ask for just a few.'"

Elisha's guidance for the widow to seek out empty jars from her neighbors offers a profound lesson in leveraging what's already within reach. This wasn't a grand plan spanning months or years; it was actionable advice rooted in the immediate—using resources close at hand. Elisha's command, "Don't ask for just a few," suggests a preparation for abundance, pushing the widow beyond the apparent scarcity marked by a single jar of oil. This story illustrates a pivotal shift from viewing our resources through a lens of limitation to seeing potential abundance.

Here's where it gets interesting and a bit counterintuitive, especially considering the widow's initial reaction. Knowing the modest amount of oil she possessed, her logic might dictate gathering only a few jars. Yet, Elisha prompts her towards faith oversight, encouraging an expectation of abundance. This moment is a call to faith, urging us to prepare for more than we can see or understand. It challenges us to rethink our own 'jar collecting' strategies in life. Are we limiting our collection based on what we think we have, or are we preparing in faith for the abundance we cannot yet see?

Moreover, the narrative resonates with a relatable truth: what we perceive as enough may not align with God's plan of abundance for us. This insight is akin to those moments that make you pause and ponder, "Hmm." It's a revelation of sorts, showcasing that our perception of sufficiency is often dwarfed by God's grand design. The widow's story is not just about oil or jars; it's a metaphor for life's potentialities when we act in faith, guided by divine instruction. It's an echo of the abundance mindset, compelling us to consider, "What if there's more prepared for us, just beyond our current belief?" Truly, it sounds like abundance to me.

THE PROCESS OF MULTIPLICATION

4 "Then go inside and shut the door behind you and your sons. Pour oil into all the jars, and as each is filled, put it to one side." 5 "She left him and shut the door behind her and her sons. They brought the jars to her, and she kept pouring."

Elisha's directive to the widow in verse 4, "Then go inside and shut the door behind you and your sons. Pour oil into all the jars, and as each is filled, put it to one side," unveils a deeper layer of the multiplication process. This isn't just about physical seclusion for a task; it's about spiritual preparation and focus. The act of shutting the door is symbolic, emphasizing a separation from external influences and distractions. It's an invitation to engage intimately with the divine provision, to concentrate fully on the task at hand without the noise of the outside world.

This isolation isn't just physical; it's a metaphor for the mental and spiritual concentration required when God sets us on a path. It represents a state of dedication, where the only voices that matter are those of your immediate circle and the divine. This focused environment is where miracles can manifest, away from the skepticism and interruptions of the external world.

Moreover, the widow's obedience to pour oil into all the jars, transitioning from one filled jar to the next, underscores a principle of faith in action. Each jar filled is a testament to the unseen becoming seen, the impossible made possible through faith and adherence to God's instructions. The process of multiplication here transcends the physical act of pouring oil; it's about the expansion of belief, the tangible proof that God's provision is limitless when we operate within His guidance and shut out the doubts and distractions.

The lesson extends beyond the widow's immediate need. It's a blueprint for us to follow when God gives us an assignment, our success often hinges on our ability to focus, to shut the doors on negativity and doubt, and to pour ourselves into His instructions with faith that the outcome will exceed our expectations. It teaches us that sometimes, to see God's work in our lives, we must create a space where His presence can fill every corner, undisturbed. This story is not just about oil or jars but about how God's abundance flows when we give Him our undivided attention and obedience.

LEVERAGING FAMILY FOR SUCCESS

The narrative of the widow's sons joining her in fulfilling Elisha's directive beautifully illustrates the power of collective effort within a family unit. This is not merely a tale of familial support; it's a testament to the strength that lies in unity and shared purpose. The widow, by not facing the daunting task alone, demonstrates the significant impact of involving one's family in overcoming challenges. It's a poignant reminder that while individual endeavors have their place, there's an unmatched potential in harnessing the collective energy and talents within a family.

Reflecting on my personal journey, the synergy within my family has been instrumental in our collective success. Each of my sons, through their unique contributions, has helped to expand our family's ventures, from online businesses to real estate investments. This collaborative spirit is not just about economic gains; it's about building a legacy and reinforcing the bond that holds us together.

The Bible's depiction of Abraham and his lineage serves as an enduring model for family unity and prosperity. Through collective faith and obedience, Abraham's family laid down the blueprint for generational blessings. This biblical principle of family cohesion and shared purpose is as relevant today as it was then. It underscores the idea that when families operate in harmony, focusing on a common goal, the possibilities for growth and blessings are boundless.

In essence, the journey of the widow and her sons, along with my own experiences, underscores a profound truth: when families come together, aligning their efforts towards a unified goal, they tap into a divine principle of multiplication and blessings. It's a call to revisit the foundational biblical teaching that collective endeavor within a family is not only beneficial but divinely favored for achieving extraordinary outcomes.

THE OUTCOME OF FAITHFUL OBEDIENCE

6 "When all the jars were full, she said to her son, 'Bring me another one.' But he replied, 'There is not a jar left.' Then the oil stopped flowing."

As this family was diligently working, they reached a point where all the jars were filled, prompting the mother to request another jar from her sons. They responded, "There are no more jars left." At that moment, the oil ceased to flow. This scenario illustrates how God provides amply to fill our storehouses. Imagine if she had limited herself to a few jars based on her initial assessment of the oil quantity. They might have remained in debt or faced another predicament. However, in this instance, she gathered many jars, all of which were filled, showcasing the supernatural multiplication that occurs in our endeavors when we invite God to intervene.

Reflecting on my own journey, I vividly recall when God revealed to me the potential of earning through the internet. This insight came before I decided to relinquish all my possessions, propelling me towards an unfamiliar territory with faith as my guide. I believed in the blessing God promised, yet I was still clinging to only cutting hair as my single source of income. By 2003, after selling and giving away my worldly belongings, I was left with no choice but to immerse myself fully in understanding the digital space, a commitment fueled by divine instruction. This period of seclusion, dedicated to mastering the internet, spanned over a year, eventually leading to a significant breakthrough just over two years later. This phase of my life, devoid of distractions and marked by sacrifices, ended in the creation of a lucrative online business after the supernatural meeting with the pastor son, "Rockwilder." My experience mirrors the widow's encounter with Elisha, underscoring the profound impact of divine guidance and obedience in realizing God's plan for abundance.

APPLYING THE PRINCIPLE TO MODERN DAY

7 "She went and told the man of God, and he said, 'Go, sell the oil and pay your debts. You and your sons can live on what is left.'"

This narrative not only demonstrates God's provision through obedience but also offers a blueprint for achieving financial independence and prosperity in today's world. The widow's act of selling the oil and paying off her debts, thereby securing a livelihood for herself and her sons, underscores a divine principle of debt cancellation and resource multiplication accessible to us now.

My journey into financial freedom mirrors the widow's story, highlighting the potential within the digital landscape. My venture into the internet evolved into a successful business model following divine guidance. This path led me to create websites, write books and other things which continually generate income. These endeavors underscore the value of producing assets that, once created, perpetually benefits others and brings financial return. The process is akin to the widow's oil—what was initially perceived as limited became a source of abundant provision.

Wealth Building Tip

Many people live a lifetime without creating any assets. What can you expect to be multiplied if you don't present God with any assets?

Recognizing and utilizing what is already within your grasp is crucial for transformation. This might involve talents, skills, or other resources that, when focused upon and developed, can lead to substantial wealth and value creation. This approach significantly surpasses traditional wage earning, where your contribution often benefits another's enterprise more than your own. The principle of leveraging what you have—essentially turning what's in your house (your mind, your resources, your skills, etc.) into a production hub of potential wealth—echoes through the widow's experience and my personal journey from only cutting hair and trading my time for dollars to creating businesses that leverage for me and make me money regardless of if I'm physically present or not.

Leverage Tip

When you have assets making your money instead of you making the money, it's the best form of leverage. What can you create that can possible sell one million times? Pray for insight and ask God to reveal to you.

The widow's story, culminating in her and her sons' ability to live on the surplus from the oil sale, exemplifies a supernatural multiplication effect that can occur in our businesses when we align with God's guidance. When I embraced the internet fully, dedicating myself to learning and applying online business principles, I experienced a breakthrough that led to financial abundance and the freedom to engage deeply with my family life. This alignment with divine instruction, devoid of distractions and fully committed to the task at hand, can indeed lead to a life outside the rat race.

The principle of working within your household to identify and develop resources that can offer value to the world is a pathway to wealth. It's an alternative to earning wages, where the exchange of time for money limits growth potential. Instead, by following the biblical model of producing goods or services that can be sold repeatedly, such as my experience with websites and books, one can create a sustainable income stream.

This narrative contrasts sharply with the conventional employment model, where labor benefits the employer's vision more than the employee's financial well-being. By embracing the biblical principle of leveraging household resources for production, as demonstrated by the widow and her sons, we can generate wealth and ensure ongoing prosperity. This approach not only offers a practical solution to financial constraints but also aligns with God's promise of provision and abundance.

In conclusion, the modern application of biblical principles, as illustrated by the widow's story and my personal experiences, offers a compelling argument for faith-based entrepreneurship. By identifying and cultivating the resources at our disposal, we can escape the rat race and enter into a realm of divine abundance and financial freedom. This journey is rooted in the belief that God has already provided us with everything we need to succeed; our task is to recognize, develop, and utilize these gifts in service to others and to His glory.

REFLECTION AND APPLICATION FOR CHAPTER 3: CANCELING YOUR DEBTS GOD'S WAY

As we conclude Chapter 3, it's crucial to reflect on the powerful lessons learned from the widow's story in 2 Kings 4 and consider how we can apply these insights to our lives. Below are some guided questions and exercises designed to help you explore and implement the principles of faith, resourcefulness, and divine provision in your financial journey.

DISCOVERING YOUR HIDDEN JARS

Inventory of Resources: Reflect on what 'olive oil' you currently have in your 'house.' What talents, skills, or resources might you be overlooking that God can multiply? List them.

_____
_____
_____
_____
_____
_____
_____
_____
_____
_____
_____
_____
_____
_____

Neighborly Resources: Consider the 'empty jars' you could gather from your community or network. How can you leverage the support or resources of those around you to fulfill God's plan for your prosperity? Identify at least three potential 'jars' you can seek out.

HERE ARE THREE EXAMPLES TO HELP JOG IDEAS FOR WHAT YOUR 'JARS' MIGHT BE:

1. **Community Skills Exchange:** Look into local or online communities where skills and services are exchanged rather than paid for with money. For instance, if you're skilled in web design, you could offer your services in exchange for someone else's marketing expertise to promote your business. This exchange not only enriches your own project but strengthens community bonds.

2. **Crowdfunding Platforms:** Platforms like Kickstarter or GoFundMe can be modern-day 'jars' where you gather financial support for a project or cause. Present your vision clearly and compellingly to attract backers who believe in your mission. This can be particularly effective for launching new products, services, or community projects.

3. **Educational Resources:** Many educational institutions and online platforms offer free or low-cost courses and workshops. By enhancing your knowledge and skills in areas relevant to your goals, you're effectively filling your 'jars' with

valuable oil that can fuel future endeavors. Websites like Coursera, edX, or local community colleges could be starting points.

KEY CONCEPTS TO REVISIT

- **Divine Strategy for Debt Cancellation:** God's ways often defy conventional wisdom. Reflect on how the widow's obedience to Elisha's unusual instructions led to her debt cancellation. How might God be directing you to unconventional strategies for overcoming your financial challenges?
- **The Principle of Multiplication:** The widow's small jar of oil was multiplied to fill many jars. How can you apply this principle of multiplication to your financial resources or talents?

FAITH ACTION STEPS

Develop a plan detailing specific actions you'll take to utilize your 'olive oil.' This could involve starting a small business, using a talent for community service, or other creative applications of your resources.

_____
_____
_____
_____
_____
_____
_____
_____
_____
_____
_____
_____
_____
_____
_____
_____

_____

_____

_____

_____

_____

_____

_____

_____

_____

_____

_____

_____

_____

_____

_____

_____

These examples represent just a few ways you can seek out 'jars' to fill with your 'oil,' leveraging what you have in a way that multiplies its value and brings you closer to achieving your financial and personal goals.

REFLECTION

This chapter invites us to trust in God's provision and to look beyond our immediate perceptions of scarcity. By embracing the lessons of faith, obedience, and creative resourcefulness demonstrated by the widow, we can navigate our way out of financial hardship and into a place of abundance and debt freedom according to God's principles.

Engaging with these exercises and reflections opens the door to experiencing God's supernatural provision in our lives. As you ponder these questions and undertake the suggested activities, may you be inspired to see beyond your current limitations and step into the fullness of God's provision and blessings for your life.

CHAPTER 4

MULTIPLICATION AND LEVERAGING RESOURCES

THE FEEDING OF THE 5,000 (MATTHEW 14:13-21; MARK 6:31-44; LUKE 9:10-17; JOHN 6:5-14)

With only five loaves and two fish, Jesus feeds a crowd of 5,000 men, plus women and children. This remarkable event, recounted in all four Gospels, underscores Jesus' mastery over physical necessities and resources. It teaches us about God's capacity to expand our limited offerings to not only fulfill our needs but to abundantly cater to others as well.

As one becomes well-versed in the Gospels, it's evident that Jesus performed numerous miracles. Each is significant within the Gospel narrative, showcasing what our Savior is capable of. Yet, they also symbolize what He can accomplish in our lives. Specifically, the miracle of feeding the 5,000 is a profound lesson in the power of multiplication.

Many of us aspire to wealth or desire more time freedom but seldom position ourselves where something we generate can be multiplied. Multiplication might manifest through a system we employ, a product we develop, or an invention that meets a widespread need. Regardless of the medium, product, or service originating from us, it must possess the potential for multiplication.

Reflecting on my time as a barber, which was my sole profession at one time, I realized I couldn't earn beyond the hours I worked cutting hair. While there's inherent value in being a tradesperson or providing a service that relies on personal skill, it's crucial to recognize that this model requires one's constant presence for income generation. Our Savior, Jesus Christ, was a carpenter—a profession demanding hands-on effort. Very respectable trade. However, when it was time to start his ministry and impact the multitudes, He had to make a transition to then follow new principles to meet His objectives to reach the masses. When considering income production and wealth building, it's essential to explore beyond direct labor, to then use systems that allow for leverage and multiplication. Jesus understood this well as its revealed in scripture how He grew His ministry from

12 individuals to the multitude of Christians that we have today.

Before going deeper into the concepts of leverage and multiplication as means to wealth creation, let's examine the multiplicative and leveraging effect Jesus demonstrated through the feeding of the 5,000. This miracle not only highlights His divine authority but also serves as a metaphor for the potential within us to significantly impact our world through what we have, no matter how small it may seem.

Focusing on John's Gospel

Now, although I listed all four Gospels in which this story occurs previously, I will be turning my attention to where the story is told by John, located at John 6:5-14. John's Gospel offers a bit more insight and details of the interaction between Jesus and the disciples.

The Role of Questions in Teaching

John 6:5-6 "When Jesus looked up and saw a great crowd coming toward him, he said to Philip, 'Where shall we buy bread for these people to eat?' He asked this only to test him, for he already had in mind

what he was going to do." A few times in the Bible, you will see that God asks questions to individuals. It happened in the Garden of Eden, where God asks Adam, 'Where are you?' It's not that God doesn't know where you're at; it's more of a question so that you could actually do an assessment of what you know or what you don't know so you can have a teachable moment. Because if somebody asks you a question and you have to think about it or give them an actual response, it's more impressionable on your mind where you will get a lesson out of it. If someone doesn't ask you a question and they simply just take care of the situation or bypass you, it's not a very teachable moment. Think about what happens in the classroom; the teacher asks students questions all day long. Do we really think that we're in front of a teacher that doesn't know the answer already? That's what we have here when we look at Jesus asking Philip a very simple question as he observed the people in the crowd coming towards him. Verse 6 actually says he asks this only to test him, for he already knew in his mind what he was going to do.

Philip answered him, 'It would take more than half a year's wages to buy enough bread for each one to have a bite!' The great thing about testing from the Lord is that it will really show you how you think, your perspective on the situation, and how you view different issues that you are faced with. I believe this line of questioning actually helps the individual who's being questioned so that they can look more closely at the situation or observe the ultimate outcome to learn a lesson that will be impressionable so they won't do it again or so they can handle the situation a lot better when it comes.

Philip's reply that it would take more than half a year's wages to buy enough bread for each one of the people to have a bite reveals his current state of mind, not fully understanding what our Savior was capable of doing not only for the people but for him as well.

Another interesting fact is to know that Philip's assessment of how much it would cost to feed all those people would be half a year's wage. So, this was no small task; this was actually something that would be extreme because we all know, regardless of the time that we're in, half a year's wage could be a significant amount of money to spend when you're talking about buying food for 5,000 people. But I believe Jesus, the master teacher, was at work even before this encounter presented itself.

ANDREW AND THE BOY'S CONTRIBUTION

John 6:8 Another of his disciples, Andrew, Simon Peter's brother, spoke up, 'Here is a boy with five small barley loaves and two small fish, but how far will they go among so many?' The reason why I chose to read the book of John is that the other Gospels don't specify that the little boy here was the one who had the barley loaves and the two fish, so this gives us an idea of where these resources came from. Now Andrew, another one of Jesus' disciples, recognizes that this little boy has five loaves and two fish but doesn't think it's sufficient enough to feed so many, so he asks the question, 'How far will this go amongst all these people?' I can't speak to what Andrew's mindset and perspective grew to be after the fact, but right here in this illustration, he's basically close-minded to the possibilities of multiplication. For one, right in the midst of him, he's completely unaware that he's walking with Jesus. A lot of times, us as Christians, we don't recognize the power of what God is and what God has and who He is to us. As I mentioned a few chapters ago, Jesus is a partner with us, so when we dedicate whatever we're doing with Him, and it's on a mission to bring value to other people in His name, He's willing to multiply whatever that thing is for the benefit of His own glory and His people.

Now, with both Philip and Andrew expressing their own human limitations and lack of optimistic thoughts in reference to what Jesus could do, Jesus has now set the stage to show a lesson that has gone down in history forever: feeding the 5,000. Jesus said, **John 6:10-11 'Have the people sit down.' There was plenty of grass in that place, and they sat down (about five thousand men were there). Jesus then took the loaves, gave thanks, and distributed them to those who were seated as much as they wanted. He did the same with the fish.**

Resourcefulness Tip
In your own life, recognize the abundance hidden within the seemingly mundane—much like the two fish and five loaves. Our limited perspectives often blind us to the potential for multiplication and wealth building right in front of us. The

story of these humble provisions teaches us a profound lesson: with a shift in perspective, what seems small can lead to miraculous outcomes. Jesus demonstrated how responsibility and resourcefulness can turn everyday items into blessings for many. So, don't overlook the significance of this story. Through prayer and gratitude, God can unveil the abundant opportunities around you, capable of feeding thousands. Embrace the truth that with God, even the smallest resources can be multiplied beyond measure. Embracing gratitude in all circumstances aligns with godly wisdom, recognizing that challenges can foster growth and resilience. So, next time you face adversity, choose to give thanks—it's a transformative act that can empower and uplift you.

THE MIRACLE OF MULTIPLICATION

Now, we get to see Jesus' present to us the process of multiplication. Jesus simply took the loaves that the little boy had, and the first thing he did after he had everyone get organized was, he gave thanks. You have to understand that the first thing you have to do is give thanks. Jesus lifts up the bread and gives thanks. It's a critical thing to give thanks for everything and for every situation; **1 Thessalonians 5:18,** says, **"Give thanks in**

all circumstances; for this is the will of God in Christ Jesus for you.

> ### *Gratitude Tip*
> *While it's natural to give thanks when everything is going well, true gratitude extends to moments of adversity. Often, we perceive challenges as solely negative, attributing them to either God or the enemy. Yet, acknowledging that God oversees both good and bad can shift our perspective. Embracing gratitude in all circumstances aligns with godly wisdom, recognizing that challenges can foster growth and resilience. So, next time you face adversity, choose to give thanks—it's a transformative act that can empower and uplift you.*

The third thing that we could observe in this text is that Jesus can take your very small thing and get it out to all the people that really need what you provide, whether it be information, whether it be some type of service, whether you're putting value in a particular product, maybe it's a book that you have already assessed that 5,000 people need. But the key principle here is to know that something that is outside of you can be multiplied if the demand is there for what you are serving. And I definitely want you to know that these people were hungry. So, it really didn't matter what type of food was going to be presented; the key was, what appeared to look like a limited supply, God comes in and does what's natural to multiply it for us, and then what was naturally only two fish, and five loaves supernaturally becomes what feeds everybody.

When they had all had enough to eat, he said to his disciples, **John 6:12-13 'Gather the pieces that are left over. Let nothing be wasted.' So, they gathered them and filled twelve baskets with the pieces of the five barley loaves left over by those who had eaten.** When you look at verses 12 and 13, you see that everyone had plenty of food; there was enough to go around, so much so that there were leftovers. Jesus told them to gather the pieces of leftovers and let nothing be wasted because we don't have a wasteful God. He's going to come in when you need Him to if you do your homework. And what I mean by homework is whatever you have in your hand to bring value to others, make sure that there's a strong enough need, so when you present it, everyone will partake of it, and your wealth will be multiplied because of what you supplied to the masses.

In the stories that I've already shared in the previous chapters, plus this story about the 5,000 being fed, we can see how Jesus used leverage and multiplication to get the desired result for the widows and for the people who were hungry. God takes small things and multiplies them into big things. Our connection with Him actually enhances when we give thanks for what those things are going to do, adding value to the lives of others as well as ourselves. But once you see things like this, you should then be able to pick it up everywhere, to understand how God works and how God grows things. I'll go further in explaining in the following.

LESSONS FROM JESUS' MINISTRY AND DISCIPLESHIP

At the age of 30, Jesus embarked on His public ministry and began to gather His disciples. The tales of Jesus and His twelve disciples, along with their numerous encounters, are well-known to many of us. The essence of sharing this is to highlight that Jesus devoted three years to training His disciples prior to His ascension to sit at the right hand of the Father, having fulfilled His mission of redeeming humanity. The critical insight here is the establishment of a multiplication system by Jesus, a concept often overlooked yet pivotal when understood. This principle, when applied to our lives, has the potential to usher in wealth in various forms, contingent on how we implement similar systems in our lives. Our God is a master strategist, offering profound lessons in His actions.

Throughout these three years, Jesus not only imparted wisdom to His disciples but also prepared them for the advent of the Holy Spirit, who would indwell them following His departure. Jesus assured them that the Holy Spirit would guide them into all truth, marking His physical absence from the earth but ensuring His Spirit remained within us. This act of Jesus signifies God's perpetual presence and operation in our lives, emphasizing the strategy of multiplication He physically initiated.

The multiplication I refer to involves Jesus educating His disciples to then deploy them in pairs across the globe, commissioning them to evangelize and replicate what they had learned during their time with Him. This method was not about reaching thousands directly but about meticulously training 12 individuals who, through a ripple effect of partnering and teaching others, would exponentially increase the number of believers. This strategic approach has led to millions embracing salvation through Christ, showcasing an unparalleled model of spiritual and numerical growth.

From this, we gather several lessons: First, the realization that Jesus, God incarnate, chose to work intimately with a select group, thereby setting a precedent for reaching the masses. He crafted a precise system of baptizing, commissioning, and spreading the gospel globally, a model no one has used more effectively to this day. Christianity's unique expansion, driven by voluntary conversion rather than coercion, contrasts sharply with other religions that dictate adherence based on birth or regional demographics. The love and grace of Jesus Christ have drawn countless individuals to Christianity, a testament to a system established thousands of years ago that continues to flourish and multiply effectively.

Leverage Tip

Many navigate life without tapping into the power of leverage—a force that drives multiplication. Jesus exemplified strategic leveraging, establishing a system perpetually advancing His mission for the Gospel. This principle isn't exclusive to spiritual realms; it's a cornerstone of wealth creation and business success. By

> *harnessing leverage, individuals propel their impact beyond personal capacity. Consider yourself: as a Christian spreading the Gospel, you're an asset in Jesus' mission, amplifying its reach through time. Leverage isn't merely a business tactic; it's a universal principle of exponential growth.* ***Are you maximizing leverage to magnify your impact and harvest greater rewards with your assets?***

THE IMPORTANCE OF SYSTEMS IN MULTIPLICATION

What could we learn from this? Well, we definitely can learn that we should have a system and organize so that what we are putting out into the world can multiply. For us, this could be our marketing or promotional strategies; this could be our training strategies and how we train others, as well as recruit others into our business or concepts; this could be how we organize our presentations for our particular product so others can read it and run with it. There are multiple things that we can learn from our Savior.

REFLECTION QUESTIONS FOR CHAPTER 4: MULTIPLYING YOUR RESOURCES

Identify Your Five Loaves and Two Fish: Reflect on what you currently have in your life that might seem small or insignificant but has the potential to be multiplied. How can you offer this to God and ask for His multiplication?

Assessment of Needs: Think about the "crowds" in your life that need feeding. This could be your family, community, or a specific group you're passionate about helping. What are their needs, and how can what you have meet those needs, even if it seems insufficient?

_____
_____
_____
_____
_____
_____
_____
_____
_____
_____
_____
_____

Faith in Multiplication: When have you experienced a situation where your resources were not enough to meet a need, but through faith and action, the situation turned around? Reflect on this moment and consider how you can apply this trust in God's provision to future challenges.

_____
_____
_____
_____
_____
_____
_____
_____
_____
_____
_____
_____
_____
_____

Organizing for Distribution: Jesus organized the crowd before distributing the loaves and fishes. How can you organize your resources, efforts, and plans to ensure maximum impact and efficiency in meeting the needs around you?

_____
_____
_____
_____
_____
_____
_____
_____
_____
_____
_____
_____
_____

Giving Thanks for Small Beginnings: Just as Jesus gave thanks for the loaves and fishes before they were multiplied, how can you cultivate a habit of gratitude for the resources you currently have, no matter how small they might seem?

Gathering the Leftovers: After Jesus fed the 5,000, the disciples gathered twelve baskets of leftovers. How can you ensure that the blessings and resources that flow from your actions are not wasted but are instead used to further God's kingdom?

_____
_____
_____
_____
_____
_____
_____
_____
_____
_____
_____
_____

Journaling Prompt: Write about a time when you felt like you only had "five loaves and two fish" and how God used it in ways you didn't expect. Reflect on what you learned from that experience.

_____
_____
_____
_____
_____
_____
_____
_____
_____
_____
_____
_____
_____
_____

Action Plan Template: Create an action plan on how you can multiply a specific resource or talent you have. Include steps for how you will offer it, organize your efforts, execute your plan, and give thanks throughout the process.

_____
_____
_____
_____
_____
_____
_____
_____
_____
_____
_____
_____
_____
_____

Prayer Guide

Heavenly Father,

First, I come before You with a heart full of gratitude. Thank You for Your unfailing love, provision, and the countless blessings You pour into my life, even those I may not always recognize. As I stand in Your presence, I seek Your guidance to open my eyes to the resources You've entrusted to me. Help me see beyond the surface, to recognize even the smallest of my offerings can be multiplied in Your hands for Your glory.

Lord, grant me the courage to offer up these resources to You, no matter how insignificant they may seem. Whether it's time, talents, or treasures, I lay them at Your feet, willing to be used as a vessel for Your purposes. In moments of doubt or fear, remind me of the miracles You've performed, of how You fed the 5,000 with just five loaves and two fish. Let those stories embolden my heart, knowing You are the same God today.

I ask for faith, Father, a faith that does not waver. As I give what I have, help me trust in Your divine multiplication. Teach me to not only look for the harvest but to trust in the process, understanding that Your ways are higher than mine. When I'm tempted to count my resources as too small, remind me that in Your kingdom, nothing is wasted, and everything is purposeful.

Please direct my steps as I use these resources. Show me where they are needed most and how I can serve Your kingdom. Align my actions with Your will, ensuring that what I do brings hope, spreads love, and glorifies Your name.

Thank You, Lord, for hearing my prayer. I wait in expectation for the amazing works You will do, not just in my life but through my life, as I offer up what I have to You. I pray all this in the precious name of Jesus,
Amen

CHAPTER 5

THE WISDOM OF MENTORSHIP

One of the most pivotal steps you can take to extract yourself from the rat race is to secure a mentor. Finding mentors is relatively straightforward, yet the manner in which you engage with them can significantly influence the effectiveness of the relationship. There are specific actions you should embrace and others you should avoid when seeking mentorship.

Primarily, it's crucial not to solicit your mentor for favors or financial support. The essence of seeking a mentor is to learn, acquiring wisdom and insight into the domain you're eager to excel in. To earn the respect of your mentor, it's imperative to avoid appearing overly dependent. While individual circumstances may vary, adopting the strategies I'll outline could simplify the process, provided your approach with humility and a genuine eagerness to learn from someone who has achieved success in your area of interest.

My First Millionaire Mentor

One of the first millionaire mentors I had the privilege of being around was my landlord, David Gong. At the age of 18, I was introduced to him because of a situation arising from my work as a barber. David owned the building where I cut hair. The owner of the barbershop stopped paying rent, and David, being the landlord, approached me to inquire about the situation. I informed him that I hadn't seen the owner for about a month. He then revealed that the owner was over four months behind on rent and would likely face eviction.

This situation presented an opportunity for me. Upon learning the amount of rent owed, which was three times less than what I was paying to the barbershop, I proposed to David that I could cover the rent. He agreed and proceeded with the legal eviction process. Eventually, I took over the shop.

This experience marked the beginning of my mentorship with David. He owned a building with about 13 stores, generating significant monthly income from a fully paid-off property. I learned invaluable lessons from him, with leverage being one of the first principles he imparted to me. When I came into some money later on, I sought David's advice on how to use it. He emphasized the importance of leveraging funds rather than spending them wastefully or on singular purchases.

At the age of 18 and 19, David's wisdom profoundly influenced my mindset and laid the foundation for my future endeavors. It guided my entrance into the internet business, where I learned to leverage my time and efforts to generate millions. Additionally, David's insights inspired me to pursue another dream of owning my own commercial building. A goal I have since achieved.

Mentorship in the Bible

The Bible offers numerous examples of mentorship, which I intend to explore to highlight the significance of having a mentor in your life. Throughout my journey, I've been fortunate to have several mentors, who have guided me in various aspects of personal and professional development. Your role is to actively listen and soak up as much knowledge and information as possible. This way, when you transition from being under your mentor's wing, you'll possess the necessary training and insights to thrive in your chosen field.

Now, I'd like to delve into the biblical mentor-mentee relationship between Elijah and Elisha. As we commenced this book discussing these two figures—both prophets, with one succeeding the other—it's pertinent to examine what lessons were derived from their interaction and how we can apply these learnings, given their mentorship dynamic illustrated in the Bible. Following we will also explore the relationship between Moses and Joshua and Paul and Timithy.

MENTOR-MENTEE RELATIONSHIP BETWEEN ELIJAH AND ELISHA

The mentor-mentee relationship between Elijah and Elisha, as depicted in the Bible through 1 Kings 19:19-21 and 2 Kings 2:1-15, serves as a prime example of the profound impact a mentor can have on an individual's life. This narrative not only illustrates the transfer of wisdom and spiritual insight from mentor to mentee but also showcases the value of mentorship in accelerating personal and professional development. Here are the key advantages and insights derived from this relationship:

Advantages Bestowed by the Mentor:

- Spiritual Inheritance: Elisha received a double portion of Elijah's spirit, symbolizing the transfer of spiritual authority and power. This was not merely a testament to Elisha's faithful service but also an empowerment that prepared him for his future role.
- Witnessing Miracles: Elisha had the opportunity to observe Elijah perform miracles, providing him with firsthand experience of divine power in action. This exposure not only solidified his faith but also served as practical learning for his own ministry.
- Teachings and Prophetic Insight: Through his close association with Elijah, Elisha gained deep prophetic insights and teachings that would be invaluable in his later service as a prophet.

Utilization and Benefits for the Mentee:

- Performing Greater Works: Armed with the double portion of Elijah's spirit, Elisha went on to perform more miracles than his mentor, including healing the sick and parting the Jordan River. This illustrates how mentorship can equip mentees to surpass their mentors in achievements.

- Leadership and Influence: Elisha's role as Elijah's successor meant he inherited not just spiritual power but also leadership over the sons of the prophets. His mentorship under Elijah prepared him for this responsibility, enabling him to lead effectively.
- Spiritual Authority: The mantle passed from Elijah to Elisha symbolized the transfer of spiritual authority. Elisha's acceptance and use of the mantle demonstrated his readiness to step into his mentor's role, showing how mentorship can prepare individuals for leadership positions.

CONNECTION FORMATION:

The connection between Elijah and Elisha was divinely orchestrated, with Elijah being directed by God to anoint Elisha as his successor. Elisha's willingness to leave his previous life and follow Elijah highlights the importance of commitment in a mentor-mentee relationship.

KEY POINTS:

- Willingness to Serve: Elisha's service to Elijah before becoming his successor teaches the importance of humility and service in mentorship. Serving as a foundation for learning and growth.
- Inheritance Beyond Skills: The double portion of spirit received by Elisha signifies that mentorship is not just about skill transfer but also about inheriting character, wisdom, and spiritual depth.
- Preparation for Greater Tasks: The mentorship prepared Elisha for tasks that would require not just the skills he observed but also the spiritual depth he inherited, demonstrating mentorship's role in preparing mentees for their future roles.

Elijah and Elisha's relationship exemplifies how mentorship can significantly enhance a mentee's capabilities, equip them for future challenges, and accelerate their journey towards achieving their goals. It underscores the mentor's role in imparting wisdom, experience, and spiritual insights, and the mentee's role in actively learning, serving, and preparing for their eventual leadership roles.

MENTOR-MENTEE RELATIONSHIP BETWEEN MOSES AND JOSHUA

The mentor-mentee relationship between Moses and Joshua, detailed in the books of Exodus, Numbers, and Joshua, stands as a compelling example of effective mentorship and its impact on leadership transition within a biblical context. This dynamic partnership not only facilitated the successful transfer of leadership from Moses to Joshua but also underscored the critical role mentorship plays in preparing individuals for significant roles. Here's an analysis of the advantages, utilization, connection formation, and key points from this relationship:

ADVANTAGES BESTOWED BY THE MENTOR:

- **Leadership Skills:** Under Moses' guidance, Joshua developed key leadership skills that were crucial for leading the Israelites into the Promised Land. Moses' leadership provided a model for Joshua to emulate, encompassing decision-making, faith, and resilience.

- **Spiritual Growth:** Joshua's spiritual maturity grew as he served under Moses. He witnessed Moses' intimate relationship with God, his steadfast faith, and his dedication to following God's commandments, which deeply influenced Joshua's own spiritual journey.

- **Strategic Military Experience:** Joshua served as a military leader from a young age, most notably leading the Israelites to victory against the Amalekites. This experience, coupled with Moses' mentorship, honed Joshua's strategic and tactical abilities, preparing him for future military challenges.

UTILIZATION AND BENEFITS FOR THE MENTEE:

- Successful Leadership Transition: Joshua's seamless transition into Moses' leadership role was a direct result of the mentorship he received. His preparedness ensured continuity and stability, guiding the Israelites faithfully after Moses' death.
- Implementing Strategic Conquests: Armed with military prowess and strategic insight gained under Moses, Joshua successfully led the Israelites in the conquest of Canaan, fulfilling the divine mandate given to Moses.
- Upholding Spiritual and Moral Laws: Joshua's adherence to the laws and commandments taught by Moses was instrumental in his leadership. His

commitment to God's directives maintained the spiritual and moral integrity of the Israelite community.

CONNECTION FORMATION:

Joshua was selected by Moses from the tribe of Ephraim as his aide, a role that facilitated close interaction and direct mentorship. This relationship was characterized by mutual respect and trust, with Joshua often accompanying Moses on important occasions, such as his visits to the tent of meeting.

KEY POINTS:

- The Importance of Proximity in Mentorship: Joshua's constant presence by Moses' side allowed him to learn through observation and direct instruction, highlighting the value of closeness in mentorship relationships.
- Preparation for Leadership: The comprehensive mentorship Joshua received under Moses equipped him not only with the skills needed for leadership but also with the spiritual depth and moral fortitude to lead effectively.

- Legacy and Succession Planning: Moses' intentional mentorship of Joshua serves as an exemplary model of succession planning, ensuring that leadership qualities, spiritual values, and mission vision are passed down to future leaders.

Moses and Joshua's mentor-mentee relationship demonstrates how deliberate and thoughtful mentorship can significantly influence a mentee's personal development, leadership capabilities, and overall success. It emphasizes the mentor's role in imparting practical skills, spiritual wisdom, and moral guidance, and the mentee's responsibility to absorb, apply, and extend this legacy.

MENTOR-MENTEE RELATIONSHIP BETWEEN PAUL AND TIMOTHY

The mentor-mentee relationship between Paul and Timothy, as depicted in the New Testament, particularly in the books of Acts, the Pauline Epistles, and the pastoral letters (1 and 2 Timothy), exemplifies a profound spiritual and ministerial bond that significantly shaped early Christian leadership and teachings. This relationship offers rich insights into the dynamics of Christian mentorship, its impact on personal growth, and the dissemination of doctrinal truths. Here's a detailed analysis of their relationship, focusing on the advantages provided by the mentor, the utilization by the mentee, the formation of their connection, and key lessons:

ADVANTAGES BESTOWED BY THE MENTOR:

- Theological Education: Paul, being a well-educated Pharisee and a staunch advocate for Christ post-conversion, provided Timothy with extensive theological education, equipping him with a deep understanding of Christian doctrine and the ability to teach others effectively.

- Ministry Skills: Under Paul's guidance, Timothy developed essential ministry skills, including preaching, teaching, and church leadership. Paul's mentorship prepared Timothy to address theological errors, conduct pastoral care, and administer church governance.

- Spiritual and Moral Guidance: Paul's mentorship extended beyond professional skills into personal spiritual and moral guidance, emphasizing the importance of personal integrity, perseverance in faith, and commitment to the Gospel's principles.

Utilization and Benefits for the Mentee:

- Effective Church Leadership: Timothy utilized the teachings and principles learned from Paul to lead the church in Ephesus effectively, addressing doctrinal issues, managing congregational disputes, and mentoring other leaders.
- Expansion of Paul's Mission: Timothy became an extension of Paul's missionary work, representing him in places Paul could not visit and continuing his work in establishing and strengthening the early Christian communities.
- Personal Growth and Legacy: Timothy's growth under Paul's mentorship is evident in his transition from a young disciple to a respected church leader, contributing significantly to the spread of Christianity and the New Testament's teachings.

CONNECTION FORMATION:

The relationship between Paul and Timothy began when Paul visited Lystra on his missionary journeys and recognized Timothy's potential and faith, which was well spoken of by the brethren. Timothy's Jewish-Christian heritage, coupled with his early faith nurtured by his mother and grandmother, made him an ideal mentee for Paul. Paul's decision to have Timothy circumcised (due to his Jewish mother and Greek father) and to take him along on missionary journeys signifies the formal start of their mentorship.

KEY POINTS:

- Mentorship Beyond Knowledge Transfer: Paul and Timothy's relationship underscores that effective mentorship involves not just the transfer of knowledge but the shaping of character and the nurturing of spiritual life.
- Importance of Faith in Mentorship: Their relationship highlights the centrality of shared faith as a foundation for mentor-mentee relationships, encouraging mentors and mentees to align their spiritual goals and values.
- Legacy Through Discipleship: Paul's mentorship of Timothy illustrates how discipleship can extend one's legacy and impact beyond personal achievements, through the empowerment and development of the next generation's leaders.

Paul and Timothy's relationship serves as a timeless model for mentorship, emphasizing the transformative power of dedicated guidance, shared faith, and mutual commitment to a higher calling. It demonstrates that mentorship, particularly in spiritual and ministerial contexts, is pivotal in personal development, the fulfillment of one's potential, and the continuation of impactful legacies.

As we progress and learn, there is an additional aspect we must grasp about engaging with God to move forward and bless others as well as receive the Lord's blessings. A prime example in the Bible that illustrates this concept is King Solomon. Solomon, the son of David, became king at a young age and was deeply devoted to the Lord. The scriptures recount how Solomon offered thousands of sacrifices to God, demonstrating his gratitude and humility. One night, God appeared to Solomon in a dream, offering him anything he desired. This scenario could tempt many, but Solomon's request altered the course of his life. As a young ruler, he sought not wealth or long life but the discernment to govern his people justly. He asked for wisdom to lead effectively without disappointing the people or God, and to maintain his connection with the Divine for guidance.

God honored Solomon's unselfish request, promising him wisdom, wealth, and longevity because he did not seek personal gain. This teaches us it's permissible to pray for our needs, aligning with the Lord's Prayer for "daily bread." The Bible encourages seeking provision without greed. Directly asking God for money might misalign with scriptural principles, as no biblical figure is documented doing so. Instead, we should seek wisdom, understanding, revelation, health, and protection to serve others effectively.

WHAT WE LEARN FROM SOLOMON

Using the principle Solomon understood—seeking wisdom from God rather than just riches—guided my approach with each mentor God blessed me with. With David, my initial mentor, I refrained from directly asking for money, despite being aware of his wealth. Instead, I seized every opportunity around him to glean knowledge and engaging in enlightening conversations. These exchanges not only enriched my understanding but also shaped my perspective on wealth and success.

Following David's mentorship, I sought guidance from several others, always prioritizing learning over monetary gain. I never approached them with requests for money but rather immersed myself in their thought processes, eager to absorb their wisdom. This approach not only facilitated my growth but also ensured that I encountered no resistance in my pursuit of knowledge.

Finding the right mentor is relatively straightforward, but it's crucial that they align with your goals and aspirations. For example, if you're looking to break into real estate, seek out experienced investors in your local community. Attend events such as auctions where they might be present. Initially, you might worry about being perceived as competition or asking for too much, but if you express a genuine desire to learn and offer assistance for free, it can be highly effective. Many individuals welcome help, and when you provide value to their lives, they may reciprocate by mentoring you. Remain open-minded and pray for guidance to connect with the right people who can support you on your journey.

Solomon's request from God illustrates the essence of how you should approach someone for mentorship. Despite his status, Solomon's humble request for wisdom to lead his people effectively was granted by God, along with unasked riches and honor. This reflects the ideal mentor-mentee dynamic: approaching with humility, seeking knowledge over personal gain, and being open to divine guidance.

In conclusion, escaping the rat race doesn't require relentless toil or mediocrity but aligning with divine wisdom and guidance. Praying for direction to fulfill your divine calling, as Solomon did, can reveal the path to making a meaningful impact on your family and community. Embrace humility and sincerity in your prayers and be prepared to follow through on the insights and opportunities God provides.

REFLECTION QUESTIONS:

1. **Identifying Your Solomon Moment**: Reflect on a time when you sought wisdom or guidance over material gain. How did that decision impact your path or outcome?

2. **Recognizing Your Resources**: Solomon understood his resource was his position and his ability to lead. What are your unique resources or talents that you might be overlooking?

_____

_____

_____

_____

_____

_____

3. **Learning from Mentors**: Think about a mentor in your life, whether formal or informal. What is the most valuable lesson you've learned from them?

_____

_____

_____

_____

_____

_____

_____

ACTIONABLE STEPS:

1. **Seeking a Mentor**: Make a list of areas in your life or career where you feel guidance could be beneficial. Begin researching individuals or communities where potential mentors might be found. Consider reaching out with specific, thoughtful questions or an offer to assist them in their work for free.

2. **Offering Your Skills**: Identify skills or knowledge you possess that could be beneficial to others. Consider how you might offer these skills in a mentorship capacity to someone else, fostering a cycle of giving and receiving knowledge.

_____
_____
_____
_____
_____
_____
_____
_____
_____
_____
_____
_____
_____
_____
_____

3. **Prayer for Wisdom**: Following the example of Solomon, dedicate time this week to pray specifically for wisdom in an area of your life where you feel uncertain or in need of guidance. Record any insights or changes in perspective that come from this time of prayer.

_____
_____
_____
_____
_____
_____
_____
_____
_____
_____
_____
_____
_____

JOURNAL PROMPTS:

1. **My Mentorship Journey**: Journal about your experiences with mentorship, both as a mentor and a mentee. What have you learned? How have these relationships shaped your approach to challenges and opportunities?

___
___
___
___
___
___
___
___
___
___
___
___
___
___
___

2. **Solomon's Wisdom in My Life**: Reflect on the concept of asking for wisdom over wealth. How can you apply this principle in your current decisions or dilemmas?

3. **A Letter to a Future Mentor**: Write a letter (you don't have to send it) to a potential mentor. Outline what you admire about their path, what you hope to learn, and how you might contribute to their work or life in return.

INTERACTIVE EXERCISE:

- **Networking for Growth**: Plan to attend a networking event, workshop, or community gathering in your area of interest within the next month. Before you go, set a goal for what you hope to learn or whom you hope to meet. After the event, reflect on any connections made and possible steps forward.

PRAYER FOR WISDOM AND MENTORSHIP

Heavenly Father,

In the quiet of this moment, I come before You with a heart open and ready to receive. I acknowledge my need for Your guidance in every aspect of my life, especially in seeking wisdom and finding mentorship on my journey.

Lord, I am reminded of Solomon, who asked for wisdom above all else. In his humility and desire to serve You faithfully, he was granted not only the wisdom he sought but also blessings beyond measure. I, too, seek that wisdom, Lord—not for my glory but for Yours. Grant me the discernment to make choices that honor You and lead me closer to the purpose You have for my life.

I also pray for guidance in finding mentors who reflect Your love and wisdom. Lead me to those who can teach me, guide me, and walk with me in understanding Your will. Help me to recognize the mentors You have already placed in my life, often in unexpected forms, and give me the courage to learn with an open and humble heart.

Teach me to be a good mentee, Lord, eager to listen, learn, and apply the wisdom shared with me. May these relationships be grounded in mutual respect, kindness, and a shared desire to grow closer to You.

And as I learn, let me also share. Equip me to be a mentor to others, sharing the wisdom and blessings You have so generously poured into my life. May I lead by example, always pointing back to You, the source of all wisdom and understanding.

Thank You, Father, for Your promise to give wisdom generously to all who ask. I trust in Your timing and Your plan, knowing that the path You have for me is filled with opportunities to grow and serve.

In Jesus' name, I pray,
Amen.

CHAPTER 6

YOUR FAITHFUL JOURNEY TO FINANCIAL FREEDOM

As we now embark on Chapter 6, there are two key focuses that I would like to share, drawn from personal experience, on navigating the journey out of the rat race. This path is not easily traversed, but with dedication, a willingness to heed the Lord's guidance, and unwavering faith, reaching your destination is entirely possible. I won't pretend that the steps required of you will be easy, but with God's grace and direction, achieving what He has shown and told you is wholly attainable.

In my early days of following the Lord and dedicating myself to whatever He blessed my hands to do, I found myself hesitating to move as quickly as I should have. I would hear God sharing insights with me, yet I didn't act as swiftly as I now wish I had. Looking back, if I had understood the full extent of His divine instruction—to give everything away for the reason He provided—I would have acted much sooner. It took me about six months to follow through with that guidance, not realizing then that His instructions come with provisions, connections, resources, and everything laid out for the path He has set before us. All we need to do is walk by faith.

Peter's miraculous catch of fish is a vivid illustration of this principle. After a fruitless night of fishing, they followed Jesus' simple command to drop their nets at a specific moment. The result was a catch so bountiful it nearly broke their nets. This act of obedience to Jesus' instructions not only provided them with an immediate, tangible benefit but also led them to follow Him thereafter. It's not explicitly stated whether they continued fishing, but Jesus' promise that they would become fishers of men signifies a redirection of their skills and efforts towards a new, divine purpose.

This narrative serves as a powerful reminder that the talents and activities we engage in currently, those we've been honing since youth, contain the seeds of what will sustain us when we place our trust in God and believe in His path for us.

Sometimes you'll receive unusual instructions from God that challenge your faith. But there's a lot God is trying to show you through these unique requirements. This is why we must **"walk by faith, not by sight" (2 Corinthians 5:7).** The world operates within a standard system, but the Lord works beyond this system, representing His kingdom's operations. We must trust that His instructions will lead us to unconventional places.

I will now highlight instances in the Bible where regular people, like you and me, received instructions to do unusual things, resulting in favorable outcomes. Sharing these stories illustrates that with God on your side, and when called to operate in faith, the situations you encounter will not be typical. Reflect on these stories from the Bible and observe how faith and obedience play crucial roles in the lives of these biblical figures.

ABRAHAM'S CALL TO SACRIFICE ISAAC (GENESIS 22:1-19):

Abraham's readiness to sacrifice his son Isaac, as commanded by God, stands as a profound testament to faith and obedience in the Bible. This trial of Abraham's faith was intense, considering Isaac was the promised son through whom his descendants were to be numbered. At the moment of sacrifice, an angel intervened, providing a ram as an alternative offering. This act of obedience and faith not only spared Isaac's life but also reaffirmed God's promise to make Abraham's descendants as numerous as the stars. This story underscores that obedience, even when it contradicts our understanding and desires, results in God's provision and the fulfillment of His promises.

GIDEON'S VICTORY OVER THE MIDIANITES (JUDGES 7:1-22):

Gideon's story teaches us about God's ability to deliver victory through faith, even when faced with insurmountable odds. Gideon, armed with only 300 men by God's command, defeated the Midianites, an enemy far greater in number. This narrative underscores that success and deliverance in our professional and personal lives do not solely depend on our resources or the scale of our network but on our obedience to God's strategy. Emulating Gideon's trust in God can inspire us to pursue our goals with the confidence that God will multiply our efforts, no matter how modest they may seem.

THE HEALING OF THE MAN BORN BLIND (JOHN 9:1-12):

This miracle performed by Jesus highlights the transformative power of faith in action. The blind man's obedience to Jesus' instruction to go and wash in the Pool of Siloam not only resulted in physical healing but also opened the eyes of many to Jesus' identity as the Son of God. This story is a metaphor for the vision and clarity we gain when we follow God's guidance, encouraging us to trust in God's plan even when the path may seem unclear or the outcome uncertain.

THE HEALING OF NAAMAN (2 KINGS 5:1-14):

Naaman, a Syrian general, was healed of leprosy after dipping in the Jordan River seven times as instructed by the prophet Elisha. His initial resistance, followed by compliance, demonstrates the victory over pride and the blessings that follow humble obedience to God's commands. This parallels the journey out of the rat race, emphasizing that surrendering our preconceptions and following God's seemingly simple or illogical instructions can lead to miraculous outcomes and healing in our lives.

ANANIAS HEALING SAUL (ACTS 9:10-19):

Ananias' role in Saul's transformation into Paul is a testament to the impact of obedience on others' destinies. Despite his reservations, Ananias followed God's command to heal Saul, a known persecutor of Christians. This act not only restored Saul's sight but also facilitated his pivotal role in spreading the gospel. This illustrates how our obedience to God's directives can contribute to larger plans we may not initially see, impacting not just our lives but those around us and beyond.

The essence of sharing these stories of faith and obedience is to illustrate that God's guidance is tailored to our individual journeys towards freedom. For instance, when God instructed me to give everything away, it was a unique directive for my path to liberation. God's instructions may vary greatly among us, as He knows precisely what each person needs to experience to attain true freedom. For some, it might mean taking a leap of faith to leave a job or endure a period of humility and sacrifice, akin to Abraham's ultimate test of faith. These acts of obedience, though they may seem unconventional or daunting, are steps towards escaping the confines of the rat race.

God's requests can push us to the brink of our comfort zones, testing our willingness to surrender fully to His will. It took me nearly two years to recover what I had given up, but the freedom and abundance I received in return were beyond measure. My success wasn't tied to a conventional job but flourished from the work I put into my websites, operated from the simplicity of a computer screen. This was the fruit of my sacrifice and unwavering trust in God's plan.

So, the pivotal question remains: Will you endure, regardless of how foolish or difficult God's instructions may seem? How deeply do you desire change in your life? Can God trust you to persevere until He brings you into your promised land? Remember, the last thing you want is to mirror the Israelites, who grumbled their way from slavery to freedom, only to long for the past due to the discomfort of transformation.

Commit to yourself and to God, right now, that you will not retreat but will follow through on whatever He instructs, leading you to financial independence and a definitive exit from the rat race. Let this chapter be a reminder and a call to faith and obedience, the bedrock upon which God can build a life of true freedom and fulfillment for you.

REFLECTIVE QUESTIONS

1. **Identifying Your Nets**: Reflect on the aspects of your life or career that you've been hesitant to pursue further due to past failures or fears. How does the story of Peter's miraculous catch inspire you to approach these areas with renewed faith and obedience to God's guidance?

2. **Contemplating Unusual Instructions**: Think of a moment when you felt God was nudging you towards an unconventional path. Did you follow through? Reflect on the outcomes or lessons learned from this experience. How does this align with the biblical instances where obedience to divine instructions led to unexpected blessings?

_____
_____
_____
_____
_____
_____
_____
_____
_____
_____
_____
_____

PERSONAL EXERCISES

1. **Journaling Exercise**: Write about a situation in your life where following God's guidance, even when it didn't make sense at the time, led to a positive outcome. If you haven't experienced this yet, describe a scenario you're currently facing where you could apply faith and obedience to see potential blessings.

---

2. **Action Plan for Obedience**: Identify one area in your life or career where you've been resistant to taking a step of faith. Outline a small, actionable plan on how you can begin to obey God's direction in this area. Include specific steps, timelines, and how you will seek God's guidance through prayer and scripture.

___
___
___
___
___
___
___
___
___
___
___
___
___
___

PRAYER POINTS

1. **Prayer for Discernment**: Pray for the ability to discern God's voice and instructions amidst the noise of the world and personal biases. Ask for the courage to follow through with obedience, even when the path is not clear.

2. **Prayer for Strength in Faith**: Request strength and perseverance in faith, especially when the instructions you receive test your limits or understanding. Pray for a heart that trusts in God's plan above your own.

CHAPTER 7

YOUR SEED CAN CHANGE YOUR LIFE

In this final chapter, I'm going to share something common amongst people who are abundantly blessed: They abundantly give. It is perplexing why giving often carries a negative connotation in the church, but many hold back on their giving, inadvertently missing the greatest blessings God has to offer.

This chapter will dive into scriptures that ignite the principle for you to receive bountifully, share my journey to wealth beyond what I thought possible through giving, and offer you an opportunity to exercise your faith as well.

Every process introduced in this book is a spiritual law. The Kingdom of God, led by King Jesus Christ himself, operates on principles distinct from worldly norms. These principles are unchangeable laws set by God, much like the law of gravity: universal, applying to all, believer, or atheist alike, because they are set in stone.

"Give, and it will be given to you. A good measure, pressed down, shaken together and running

over, will be poured into your lap. For with the measure you use, it will be measured to you." (Luke 6:38) This verse encapsulates the principle of reciprocal generosity, promising that the generosity we show will return to us in full measure.

Another of God's principles is sowing and reaping. The Bible says,

"Remember this: Whoever sows sparingly will also reap sparingly, and whoever sows generously will also reap generously." (2 Corinthians 9:6)

"Do not be deceived: God cannot be mocked. A man reaps what he sows." (Galatians 6:7)

"One person gives freely, yet gains even more; another withholds unduly, but comes to poverty. A generous person will prosper; whoever refreshes others will be refreshed." (Proverbs 11:24-25)

"Honor the LORD with your wealth, with the firstfruits of all your crops; then your barns will be filled to overflowing, and your vats will brim over with new wine." (Proverbs 3:9-10)

Your financial gift is your seed. If you find yourself facing financial roadblocks or can't achieve a breakthrough, it could be due to not making sacrificial giving a part of your life. Releasing your money and putting it into action activates a principle with God, opening up supernatural doors and making connections where you least expect them.

When I purchased my commercial building, the owner initially asked for 1 million dollars. Eight months into contract negotiations and just a month away from closing, the owner, frustrated by an extension I requested, reduced the price by $100,000 out of the blue. I didn't even ask him to do it. This unexpected blessing is just one example of how my giving has been rewarded. Let me explain why.

The week before as I was selling my home, the new buyer came up short $10,000. It was up to me to either let the deal continue or use this as a way to get out of the deal and probably get more money. We had so many offers on the home. But when we showed it to his family a few weeks before the closing, his two young sons walked up to the door and I said, "Welcome home guys." When he came up short at the closing, I remembered how happy his kids were to enter the home for the day of the showing.

So, I just gave the $10,000 up and said God will bring it back another way. That is exactly what he did a few weeks later with my commercial deal. However, he put $90,000 on top of the $10,000.

I challenge you now to sow a seed into my ministry, embracing the principle of giving. Trust in the supernatural provision and connections that follow and consider how embracing sacrificial giving can transform your financial situation and help you escape the rat race, all by adhering to God's way.

By supporting this ministry, you're invited to participate in a covenant of faith, sowing a seed with the significance of the number seven—God's number of completion. This symbolic act is meant to echo the divine order of creation, where God completed His work in six days and rested on the seventh, marking it as a time of completion and sanctity. This book comprises seven chapters, each designed to guide you towards realizing a life of financial independence and spiritual fulfillment. I presented to you 7 biblical principles that will change your life within each chapter of this book. 1) Faith, 2) Obedience, 3) Sacrifice, 4) Wisdom, 5) Resourcefulness,

6) Gratitude, 7) Generosity. Once followed will all bring you significant increase in your life.

Your act of giving is a step towards bringing the teachings and principles contained within these chapters to fruition in your life.

Sow Your 7 Seed NOW!

Multiply options for sowing your seed have been thoughtfully chosen to reflect the theme of divine completion and multiplication:

$7, symbolizing the beginning of your journey towards financial breakthrough and spiritual growth.

$77, representing an intensified commitment to trusting God's process and principles.

$777, a larger step of faith, symbolizing your readiness to receive God's abundant blessings.

$7,777, for those who feel called to make a significant impact and are ready to embrace the fullness of God's provision and favor.

Whatever level of seed you sow, expect a return. As I receive your seed, I'll pray for your harvest. But I want you to consider the level of sacrifice you're making with the seed. If $7 isn't really a sacrifice, consider going up to $77. Wherever you are, your sacrificial gift will be honored, because only the Lord knows what's a sacrifice to you. Before I gave my last $17,600, I had told my wife we were going to keep it and wait for the Lord to move, since everything else had dried up. But the Lord sent me a message while I was laying prostrate on the floor praying that He wasn't moving on my behalf because I hadn't released the $17,600 in faith when He told me months ago to give everything away. Once I was obedient and released it where He told me to plant it, within minutes, the pastor told me who her son was, I knew immediately that God came through on His promise. God is strategic in what He does, so don't hold back—step out in faith today.

HOW TO SOW YOUR SEED

As you choose to sow into this ministry, do so with the faith that God will honor your obedience and generosity, opening doors to the financial freedom you seek. This is not just an act of giving but a spiritual investment into your future, aligning your financial actions with divine principles to unlock blessings beyond measure.

As we conclude this journey through "Escaping the Rat Race," it's essential to reflect on the transformative power of faith, obedience, and generosity we've explored across these seven chapters. This book has not merely been a guide to financial independence but a spiritual voyage, inviting you to align your life with God's principles for abundance.

In sharing personal experiences, biblical narratives, and the principle of the supernatural seed, the aim has been to illustrate that true financial freedom and escaping the rat race isn't about amassing wealth through worldly means. Instead, it's about understanding and applying God's kingdom principles—faith, obedience, and generosity—to your life.

This final chapter emphasizes the act of giving as not just a financial decision but a spiritual covenant with God. By sowing your seed, you are stepping into a realm of faith where you trust God not only with your finances but also with your life's direction. The options provided for sowing your seed—**$7, $77, $777, $7,777**—symbolize a journey from initiation to a deeper, more substantial commitment to living according to God's word and promises.

As you close this book, let the principles you've learned not merely be words on a page, but seeds planted in the fertile ground of your heart. May your act of sowing into this ministry be the first step toward a life of supernatural abundance, where your financial breakthroughs serve as a testament to God's faithfulness.

Remember, God's kingdom operates on principles that are timeless and unchanging. Your willingness to align with these principles through faith, obedience, and generosity sets the stage for God to work mightily in your life, far beyond what you could ask or imagine.

May you move forward from this reading experience not as the same person who began it but as someone transformed by a deeper understanding of God's desire for your prosperity, well-being, and spiritual growth. And as you apply these teachings, may you witness the unfolding of God's supernatural provision in every area of your life.

Thank you for embarking on this journey. The path to escaping the rat race and stepping into divine abundance is before you, illuminated by the principles of faith and obedience. As you walk this path, keep your heart open to God's guidance, your hands ready to give, and your spirit attuned to the whispers of the Holy Spirit. The best is yet to come, and it starts with a seed of faith.

Blessings on your journey to financial independence and spiritual fulfillment.

Pastor Allen Brown

REFLECTION QUESTIONS

1. **Understanding Principles**: Reflect on the kingdom principles discussed throughout this book. Which principle resonated with you the most, and why?

_____
_____
_____
_____
_____
_____
_____
_____
_____
_____
_____
_____
_____
_____

2. **Personal Application**: How can you apply the principle of the sacrifice in your current financial situation? Describe a step you can take this week to act on this principle.

___
___
___
___
___
___
___
___
___
___
___
___
___

3. **Faith and Obedience**: Recall a time when you experienced the power of faith and obedience in your life. How did that experience shape your understanding of God's provision?

4. **Generosity's Impact**: How has your perspective on giving and generosity changed after reading this book? Are you more inclined to give differently, and if so, in what way?

5. **Spiritual Growth**: In what ways has this book challenged you to grow spiritually, especially in areas of trust and dependence on God?

6. **Future Steps**: Identify one financial goal you have for the next year. How do you plan to incorporate the principles learned from this book to achieve it?

INTERACTIVE ELEMENTS

Prayer of Commitment: Offer a prayer committing to trust in God's principles of faith, obedience, and generosity. Ask for guidance in applying these principles to achieve financial freedom.

Journaling Prompt: Write a letter to God expressing your desires for financial independence and how you hope to achieve it through His principles. Reflect on any specific instructions you feel God might be leading you to follow.

_____

_____

_____

_____

_____

_____

_____

_____

_____

_____

_____

Action Plan: Create a simple action plan that incorporates giving as a foundational element. This could include setting aside a specific amount for giving each month, identifying a ministry or cause you feel led to support, or finding creative ways to give of your time and talents.

_____
_____
_____
_____
_____
_____
_____
_____
_____
_____
_____
_____
_____
_____

Testimony Time: Reflect on any financial breakthroughs or blessings you have experienced. Consider sharing your testimony with your church, small group, or on social media to encourage others with the power of obedience and giving.

Conclusion

By engaging with these reflection questions and interactive elements, you're taking meaningful steps toward not just financial independence, but a deeper, more fulfilling relationship with God. Remember, the journey to escaping the rat race is not just about achieving financial success; it's about living in alignment with God's principles and experiencing the fullness of His blessings in every area of your life.

JOURNAL NOTES

_____
_____
_____
_____
_____
_____
_____
_____
_____
_____

CLOSING PRAYER

Heavenly Father,

As I close this chapter of exploration and learning, my heart swells with gratitude for the path You have guided me through. Within the chapters of this book, I've discovered seven biblical principles destined to transform my life: Faith, Obedience, Sacrifice, Wisdom, Resourcefulness, Gratitude, and Generosity. These principles, presented as the blueprint for financial breakthrough and spiritual wealth, promise a significant increase in my life when faithfully followed.

Lord, I seek Your divine strength to apply these teachings to my daily walk. Empower me to live with unwavering Faith, to act in steadfast Obedience, to embrace Sacrifice with grace, to apply Wisdom in all decisions, to approach challenges with Resourcefulness, to cultivate a heart of Gratitude, and to spread Generosity with open hands.

May these values not only guide my professional and personal journey but also reflect the depth of Your love and integrity in everything I undertake. Bless me with the clarity to see Your hand at work in my life, the courage to chase the dreams You've planted in my heart, and the joy of making a meaningful impact on those around me.

Help me to remember that true success comes not from worldly wealth but from the impact I make in the lives of others through the love, joy, and peace I share. Guide me to be instruments of Your will, bringing light and hope to those around us.

In Jesus name, I pray,

Amen.

ABOUT THE AUTHOR

Allen Brown is the esteemed pastor of Christian Believers Church, Inc., nestled in the the Poconos region of Pennsylvania. His journey with Christ began in 1998 during a transformative Easter morning service, where he committed his life to the Lord and found salvation. Drawing from a wealth of life experiences and a deep spiritual walk with Jesus Christ, Allen's insights and wisdom have been honed over the years, evident in the remarkable results he has achieved in his Christian journey.

Married for 25 years to his devoted wife, Melissa Brown, the couple shares a commitment to both their family and their ministry. Together, they have nurtured four children while tirelessly serving in various capacities within the church.

From a young age, Allen displayed entrepreneurial spirit, establishing his first business at the age of 12 and venturing into successful business dealings by 18, generating millions along the way. This entrepreneurial acumen, coupled with a passion for sharing knowledge, led Allen to become an author and the proud owner of Build Our Kingdom Publishing. Through his books and publishing endeavors, Allen aims to impart valuable teachings that not only enrich lives spiritually but also empower individuals to achieve financial freedom.

Allen attributes every success in his life to the guiding hand of God, especially during moments of adversity. Fully dedicated to serving God, Allen's ministry in Pennsylvania is marked by his commitment to teaching the gospel of Jesus Christ. He emphasizes the importance of trusting in God and applying godly principles to realize His promises.

Beyond his pastoral duties, Allen cherishes spending time with his beloved wife and their four sons. Together, they embody the values of faith, family, and service, reflecting Allen's unwavering dedication to spreading the goodness of the Lord Jesus Christ and guiding believers towards financial stewardship rooted in Godly wisdom.

ChristianBelieversChurch.org

Other Books by Pastor Al

Million Dollar Seed

How My Last $17,600

Grew to

Millions God's Way

I will Teach You How to Hear

God's Voice

What Every Christian
Should Know About
Hearing the Voice of God

30 Day to A Powerful Prayer Life

Strengthen Your Faith and
Deepen Your Connection
with God in 30 Days

Available at AllenBrownMinistries.com

www.ingramcontent.com/pod-product-compliance
Lightning Source LLC
Chambersburg PA
CBHW072159070526
44585CB00015B/1215